HER LONGEST DAY

A veteran journalist describes her husband's sudden death, her reactions, and her struggle to begin living again—to reshape her life *as a widow*. In numb and tearless grief she endured the longest day of her life, and the following days and weeks were full of details and arrangements and the heartbreaking job of disposing of personal effects. Only family, friends, her minister and her faith helped her through the ordeal.

This book, with its battle between belief and doubt, hope and despair, offers widows, their friends and counselors invaluable insights into life and death and the nourishment that Christianity gives to those who reach out to it.

ON

BECOMING

A WIDOW

(Original title: WHEN YOU'RE A WIDOW)

CLARISSA START

PUBLISHING HOUSE
St. Louis • London

ON BECOMING A WIDOW
(Original title: *When You're a Widow*)

Published by Jove Publications, Inc. for
Concordia Publishing House

Concordia edition published May, 1973
Second printing, January 1978

© 1968 Concordia Publishing House
All Rights Reserved

Library of Congress Catalog Card Number: 73-78-880

Printed in the United States of America

Concordia Publishing House, St. Louis, Missouri 63118, U.S.A.
Concordia Publishing House Ltd., London, E.C. 1, England

Contents

1. A Chapter Ends   7
2. The Longest Day   16
3. Getting Through the Ordeal   23
4. Words and the Word   29
5. Only Another Widow Understands   35
6. You Never Know   41
7. The Grisly Details   46
8. You Can't Run Away   54
9. Pulled Together—Pulled Apart   62
10. Beautiful Spring   69
11. Good Days and Bad   72
12. To Bank and to Market   77
13. Maytime   84
14. One Step at a Time   89
15. A Fifth Wheel   95
16. Parents Without Partners   102
17. The Blessing of Work   105
18. Sex and the Single Widow   110
19. The Years Ahead   116

This is a very poor start to this book, but there is much good Christian material in it

A Chapter Ends

MY HUSBAND USED TO POKE MILD FUN AT ME for my interest in those little astrological horoscopes sold at the beginning of each year. I had given up buying them, but early in January I picked up one at the beauty parlor and turned to my sign—Aries—to read the month-by-month predictions. My forecast for March began, "A long chapter of your life comes to a close."

For some reason or other, the sentence bothered me. I mentioned it to my husband, and we discussed how many chapters a life has—family, friends, professional—and how death could alter them. It never occurred to me that the chapter closed would be our almost 29 years of marriage.

It was not completely unexpected. We had known about the heart condition since the summer before. He carried tiny pills in his pocket and climbed the stairs slowly. But the doctor had said, "You can live a long time with care." He had given up smoking and yard work. Our son began carrying in the fireplace logs and the groceries. I took to slipping behind the wheel of the car when we went out. But even our close friends didn't know. Normally a quiet man, he became a little quieter.

The first Saturday in March was a day I was to relive many times in agonizing memory. It was a moist and muggy day, and I could tell that he was feeling uncomfortable. We did our usual supermarket shopping, and I called our son to carry the bags in from the car.

After I had put the groceries away, I went into the living room and put a record on the record player, a rather unusual thing for me to do on a Saturday morning. My husband followed me in.

"What are you listening to?"

"An old Mary Martin record. It's been going through my mind all week. 'Speak Low' is the song. I keep thinking of the part that goes, 'The curtain descends, everything ends—too soon, too soon.' You know?"

"Yes," my husband said. "I know."

The record was over. I stood up with a sigh. So much to do. Always so much to do. My life is everlastingly overscheduled. Whether or not you place any credence in astrology, Aries people tend to be like that, biting off so much that they choke on it.

I glanced in the hall, where my refinishing project, an old round coffee table, sat surrounded by paint remover and stain and brushes and steel wool and sandpaper. How relaxing it would be to get back to work on it. But not today. I had four speeches to make the next week, and each one had to have special notes. Two of them were to be delivered in Grand Rapids, Mich.; also one at a doctors' wives meeting where I'd been given a special topic, and one at our church, where just about everyone had heard me so I couldn't give that "same old speech."

In addition the Women's Advertising gridiron show, for which I'd written a song and skit, was having its dress rehearsals Saturday and Sunday, and I'd promised to go one of the two days. Should I go to the rehearsal today and write the speeches tomorrow? No, I couldn't relax until the speeches were out of the way. Better write them first.

"I don't know how I'll ever get through next week," I said.

I plunged into work in the back bedroom, where we

had a desk and typewriter, came out long enough for lunch, went back to work. I was aware of my husband restlessly walking around the house. In mid-afternoon he came through the room, paused at the back stairs landing.

"I suppose you're busy?" he said—hesitantly.

"Yes, I'm TERRIBLY busy"—with wifely annoyance. Then, slightly contrite, "Why—did you want something?"

"No—it's all right."

My father went to the doctor's office in the afternoon to pick up a fresh supply of tranquilizers for my mother, who was senile, and restless at night. He came back to report with annoyance that the doctor had not been at his office. That was most unusual, I said; he must be out of town. My son came in to remind me I'd promised to take him and some friends to a combo tryout at a high school in another suburb. I sighed anew.

"Maybe your father," I began. "No, he's not feeling well. I'll take you."

We were scheduled to attend a dinner that night. A longtime friend, best man at our wedding, was involved in a civil service competition for which I'd been a judge. This was the awards dinner.

"You don't have to go tonight," I said to my husband as I left. "I have to sit at the head table, but you can stay home."

"Well, I'll see," he said.

It was foggy and starting to rain as I chauffeured the boys and their guitars and amplifiers to the tryout. Another parent would pick them up, so I could go home. When I returned, my husband was sitting in the kitchen, dressed and having a cocktail.

The drink before dinner was prescribed by the doctor.

"Smoke less and drink more," he had said. "A little whiskey before dinner each night will relax you."

My husband rarely drank, and we had never had a cocktail hour before dinner except when guests were present, but we had come to enjoy the practice—less for the drink than for the opportunity it gave us to exchange the news of the day without the hubbub of family.

"You've decided to go?" I said. "You don't have to, you know."

"Yes, I feel much better." He gave a little laugh. "I can see how a person could become an alcoholic. You think, if it makes me feel this good at 5 o'clock in the evening, I might as well feel good at 10 o'clock in the morning.

"I was thinking," he continued, "about old_____," he named a lawyer who had shared office space with him in his early days. "We used to make fun of him, the way he came in and climbed a few steps and then stopped, just the way I do. And the way he smelled of liquor after lunch. We thought he was a lush. Now I know how he felt."

"Whatever happened to him?" I asked idly. I was fixing my parents' dinner.

"Oh, he's gone. Died a long time ago."

I dressed for dinner. Our friends picked us up. We had questioned the wisdom of riding with them, but I decided it would save our driving, and besides our host had promised they would leave whenever we wanted to go. My husband greeted his old friend as we got in the car.

"Irv," he said. "I decided I was going to your dinner tonight if it killed me."

The dinner was a pleasant affair. The mayor and his wife were at the cocktail party in the private room reserved for special guests. So was a radio commentator and half a dozen "big wheels" we knew. It was quite gay, and my husband was enjoying himself.

At dinner he ate very little, but neither did I. Banquet feed was no treat for people who'd been on the circuit as long as we had. The strolling musicians played at the head table and one of the guests, a big, lusty-lunged clown, requested "St. Louis Blues" and sang along so loudly that people at the end of the huge room applauded. My husband laughed and egged him on.

Dinner and the awards over, they cleared the room for dancing. I looked at my husband. He seemed drawn and tired.

"We'll sit a few minutes and then leave," I said.

I danced a dance with the colonel who was our friend's boss. We got to talking about overseas service, and I found he'd been in Iran. When we sat down, I leaned across to my husband.

"I've been telling the colonel about the Oriental rugs you bought when you were stationed in Persia," I said. "He has some too."

They turned to one another and began talking of their mutual experiences. My husband was smiling and gesticulating with animation.

"He really can be charming when he wants to be," the thought occurred to me. "He's been so cross and cranky lately, but he can really turn it on."

But I had promised we'd leave early, so I sought out our friends and made the excuses I made so often and so glibly.

"I'm a party pooper," I said (I, who could dance until dawn). "We have to teach Sunday school in the morning, and I need my rest."

We talked brightly on the way home about our week ahead. I was going to Grand Rapids on Wednesday, my husband to a Legal Aid Society meeting in Kansas City on Thursday. Our son was playing in a band concert in Cape Girardeau on Friday. What a routine! How would we ever make it through the week? But this had been fun. We must get together soon.

"Want a piece of cake?" I asked, as we paused in the kitchen.

"Ugh—cake—no."

That was funny. He loved cake. I felt an uneasy chill.

We went to bed, but he had a restless night. Nothing unusual. He always had a restless night after a late Saturday dinner. Since I had known of the heart condition I always listened when he went out to the bathroom in the middle of the night. His father had died of a heart attack in the bathroom after a big dinner, late at night. I often found myself waiting to go back to sleep until he returned.

But this particular night I slept unusually soundly, only vaguely aware that he was moving about, sitting in the chair, on the edge of the bed. The thought crossed my head that perhaps I should ask if he wanted me to call the doctor, but then I remembered; the doctor hadn't been at his office, so he must be out of town.

Sometime in the early morning I rolled over against a hard object. It was the control button of the heating pad. The cord was stretched under my back; he must have arranged it without even waking me.

"Does that bother you?" he asked. "I've got the heating pad on my chest."

"No, it doesn't bother me." Sleepily. "Can I do anything?"

"No, I'm all right."

At 7:30 in the morning a noise awakened me. Like someone snoring. Was he having a bad dream? I'd read once that nightmares could be fatal for heart patients and you should wake them. I turned.

"Gary," I said. And then with alarm, "GARY . . ."

His head jerked several times. One eye was distended. His left arm jerked up (like a puppy we'd once had—she died of a heart attack and her paw flew up just like that—the parallel struck me). And then he was still.

I leaped up, ran wildly into the hall. My parents were downstairs at breakfast. My son was sleeping. I called him.

"Bruce—come quick. Daddy's had a heart attack. I think he may be dead."

The boy came into the room, let out a cry.

"My father's dead—my father's dead."

"No. Maybe he isn't. I'll call the doctor. You wait here. Try heart massage." We had seen a program on television in which an angina victim was revived by heart massage. I dialed the doctor.

"Gary?" He sounded incredulous. "You mean Gary? Can you tell if he's still breathing? Is he blue?"

"No, he still has color." Hope rushed into me. "Would one of the nitroglycerin pills help, do you think?"

"Maybe—"

I rushed back to the bed and put a pill under his tongue, but it rolled out. I leaned down and tried mouth-to-mouth resuscitation. Nothing seemed to work.

"I'll call an ambulance," the doctor said. "We'll take him to County Hospital. I don't know if I can make it. I was just leaving for the airport, on my way to Chicago . . ."

It seemed only seconds when I heard men's voices, feet coming up the stairs. A policeman. Firemen. Equipment. One man lifted my husband's wrist. His brief expression told me everything. But they tried a bellowslike apparatus which lifted and dropped, lifted and dropped.

13

"Is there any hope?"

"He doesn't seem to be responding."

Hurriedly I threw on clothes. My son and I went to the car. They carried the stretcher outside. Neighbors were gathered in the driveway.

It seemed a million miles to the hospital. A light rain was falling. My son and I said nothing.

I parked the car at the emergency entrance, went in. A nurse directed me to a doctor's office. A foreign-looking young man in a white coat sat there. I remembered what a friend had said the night the highway patrolman woke her up. I used the same words.

"My husband is dead, isn't he?"

"Yes. Sorry to say, yes."

There were formalities. A stern-looking woman sitting at a typewriter. Asking questions that seemed impossible to answer.

"Your husband's mother's maiden name?"

"I don't remember. Let's see . . . Smith, I think it was. Yes, that was it, Smith."

"When did you last see your husband alive?"

I turned to protest—"I didn't kill him . . ."

"Why just now . . . at 7:30 . . . I mean, I saw him die."

All of this was to appear on a formidable sheet called a death certificate, which I would see many, many times, copy after photostatic copy. I signed my name, and we walked out. The fireman was still standing by the ambulance. I recognized our bed pillow.

"I can take that home if you want."

"Sure thing. It'll save me a special trip."

"Thank you, thank you for everything. I'm very grateful . . ."

"Sorry we couldn't do anything."

"There was nothing anyone could have done."

I looked at myself in the rearview mirror of the car. An appalling thought had just hit me.

"I'm a widow," I thought. "I don't look any different. But I'm a widow."

I was one of the eight million women left alone.

CHAPTER 2

The Longest Day

STUNNED AND UNBELIEVING, MY SON AND I DROVE HOME.
"Gary's dead," I said to my father, waiting at the
door.

I went to the telephone. Many times in the past year
I had rehearsed this scene, and now it was as if I were
playing out a part, as routinely as one might go
through a disaster drill.

First a call to Helen asking her to call the others of
our closest group of friends, which we called the Saturday Night Crowd. Then a call to Damon, our assistant editor, knowing he was an early riser, asking him
to call others in the office. Then a call to Dee, my husband's secretary, asking her to notify his board and
co-workers. Then a call to my Aunt Olie asking her to
notify relatives. I put off calling my husband's step-
mother and sister; they sleep late on Sundays, and it
would be a difficult call to make. I called the church to
say we would not teach Sunday school and to ask that
they announce my husband's death at services. I
called the funeral parlor.

My finger was poised at the dial for perhaps the
third or fourth of these calls when I looked up and
there stood Ed, one of the men of our Saturday Night
Crowd. Quiet, big, broad-shouldered, looking to me
like the Rock of Gibraltar. I stood up.

"Oh, thank you," I said. And collapsed against him.

But only momentarily. Looking back, I marvel at
the calm and composure with which one reacts to total
shock.

"I must do everything there is to do right away," I

thought, "before I give in to this. I must get it all done."

And so by 10:30 Ed and I were entering the rear door of the funeral parlor. There sat our assistant minister. Again I buckled momentarily, in gratitude.

I had steeled myself to be very composed in making funeral arrangements. This was a subject about which my husband had some strong convictions. He abhorred and deplored expensive funerals, and whenever he heard of a friend who said, "You can't get by for less than $2,000—that's their starting price," he would explode. Often he told of his own experience, arranging the funeral of an elderly aunt.

"There's very little insurance and she has big doctor bills," he told the man in charge. "How cheaply can you do it?"

"We start at $350," the man had said.

"You can do it, if you level with them," my husband often said. "We spent a little more than that—$500 or $600—but it can be done."

The funeral director I had chosen showed me around a room of coffins. They all looked alike. This one was $2,000—$1,700—$1,500—$1,100—$950. . . . He paused. I set my chin.

"Don't you have anything cheaper?"

"I'm afraid not. . . . Well, we do have some at $750, but they're the old-fashioned kind with octagonal ends . . . they don't use them anymore."

I smothered a smile. Fashions in coffins yet!

"Of course you'll get the $250 from Social Security," the funeral director said. "And was your husband a veteran? That's another $225 or $250—so that gives you $500 right there. . . ."

"I have two elderly parents to support and a son to send to college," I said. "We'll take the $950 one. And I want the notice in the newspapers only once for each paper. I understand that runs into money too."

"I bet he really thought I'm a cold, heartless character," I said to Ed as we left, "but I could almost hear that Scotsman, Davidson, saying, 'You better shop around a bit.'"

"You were fine," Ed said. "Don't worry about it."

Our house was filled with people when I returned. The lawyer who was my husband's assistant, offering to handle all my legal work and any other details. No charge, absolutely—"I would do it for the widow of any lawyer," he insisted. The friend who had taken us to the dinner the night before. Also a lawyer, he would take care of the government claims, he told me, the Social Security and the veterans. He would tell me what information to give him.

And then the neighbors. And the friends. A steady stream of them. Bringing cakes, casseroles, dishes of jello, straightening the house, sweeping the front porch, doing the breakfast dishes. Someone asked if I had eaten. No, come to think of it, I had not.

I sat down to my usual morning fare, bacon, eggs, toast. To my complete, utter, absolute amazement, I found myself unable to swallow a bite. I, who had eaten a hearty breakfast two hours after childbirth, even after the birth and death of a second child, after heartbreak, disappointment, defeat of all kinds, illness, anger, worry. It had always been my boast that nothing ever took my appetite away. I had never known what it was to be "too sick to eat," "too upset to eat."

This was my first encounter with the physical effects of emotional shock and grief. I simply could not eat. I threw the food away.

But if the dark waters of tragedy engulfed me, the warm waves of love washed over me. The friends who came to the door and simply took me in their arms. My son's godmother, who took him to his room to comfort him. When I tried to choke out my thanks, one friend said: "We're all just standing in a circle, you know—holding hands."

The phone began to ring. People had heard the news at church, over the radio. The commentator who had attended the dinner with us sounded as if he were in tears. "I saw him just last night," he had said.

The radio—I was galvanized into action again. I hadn't thought it would be on radio. I couldn't let my sister-in-law and mother-in-law hear it that way. I would have to call them immediately. It was not an easy call, but they took it well.

There was more to do. Get it done immediately. Ed took me downtown to my office, where I asked the watchman to let me into the file room (the newspaper "morgue") to find the recent picture my husband had liked, so they wouldn't use the old one he didn't like. I typed out a skeleton of facts for his obituary. How often I had done this for friends! I put in a long-distance phone call to the women's clubs in Grand Rapids. At first I had considered keeping my commitment.

"It's good for you to keep busy," Ed had said, "but I think you had better consider whether or not you'll be able to make a speech a day after the funeral."

It was the make-up-your-mind way my husband had always advised me. I agreed I had better cancel all my dates.

I bundled up unanswered mail, bills that would be due within the week, unfinished business of all kinds, took it to the car.

We had discussed the subject of cemetery lots only a few weeks earlier with my aunt and uncle. I had not been thinking of my husband at the time but of my mother, in her 80s and not well. My uncle had told me he had extra lots in two cemeteries; I could choose.

The rain was coming down steadily as we drove to the first cemetery. It was in an out-of-the-way place, down a series of side streets, not a prominent or a fashionable location. ("How did she ever pick a place like this?" Would people say that?)

We turned in the drive, and straight ahead was a quaint Victorian building . . . almost unreal, standing there in the rain.

"Gary would have loved it," I said. "He loved old buildings."

The driveway skirted a lovely lake. Swans skimmed the edge, seeking shelter from the rain. There were trees and hills. The road was not very good, but already I had made up my mind.

"I know the other place," I said. "It's on a main thoroughfare. It's very nice and convenient, but let's not bother going there. Gary can't choose, but I can—and I want to be buried here."

We drove quickly past and through the other cemetery, but the decision was the same. And for the first time that day I felt a small sense of contentment.

It was late afternoon, and the house was still crowded with people. One friend, a brusque and salty-tongued newspaperman, bustled in.

"I told myself I wouldn't come over," he said, "so here I am!"

"Try to eat something," they said to me. I swallowed a little jello. For two or three days, jello was all I could eat. I recommend it as an offering to the bereaved, although the spaghetti and the cakes and pies and fried chicken were useful in feeding others.

"You must get your rest," they said too.

And suddenly the house was empty. My parents in bed. My son and I in the living room.

"It seems funny," he said, "with everyone gone. Kind of lonely."

"Yes," I said. "I couldn't wait for them to leave, and now I wish they hadn't left."

"Do you mind if I watch the FBI show on TV?"

"No, of course not."

But I couldn't watch. I walked to the back door. The lights of a car. Thank goodness. Company. The couple we'd been with the night before. And—of all things—it was snowing. The ground was white.

They visited. And then they, too, were gone. And I turned out the lights and went upstairs to the bedroom. We have a big antique bed with four big pillows. It was an idea we'd acquired from European travel.

"I like this idea of having two pillows apiece," my husband had said in a German hotel in the Bavarian Alps. "Why don't we get some extra pillows when we get home?"

Just a few weeks before his death he had suggested that I use the accumulated Eagle Stamp books, some $30 worth, to buy new pillows. They were goose feather pillows, beautiful big downy ones. And he had died on one.

There it sat. A white mountain in the dark room. How could I ever get into that bed? How could I ever sleep? I looked around, terrified, wanting to run and hide. I glanced at the night table. There was the Bible.

I undressed, found my reading glasses, gingerly eased into my side of the bed, still looking out of the corner of my eye at the large pillow. I opened the Bible at random.

The Gospel According to John, Chapter 14. That was where the Bible opened, and this is what I read: "Let not your heart be troubled; ye believe in God, believe also in Me. In My Father's house are many mansions; if it were not so, I would have told you. I go to prepare a place for you. . . ."

On and on went the beautiful, familiar words. And something kept me reading, on and on through less familiar words, until I had reached the 18th verse:

"I will not leave you comfortless; I will come to you."

I turned out the light and lay in the darkness. There was no sleep all that night. But there was no fear either.

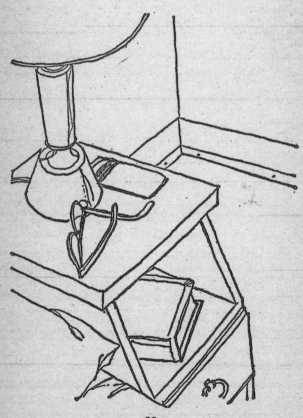

CHAPTER 3

Getting Through the Ordeal

FRIENDS AND FAMILY GATHER AROUND TO HELP A WIDOW over what they assume will be the worst part of the ordeal, the funeral parlor visitation and the burial. It is true that some women find the traditional formalities an impossible achievement. Some break down at the first sight of the man in the coffin, others at the graveside. Some—especially those who have had an exhausting, emotion-draining experience with long illness—are unable to attend the last rites at all.

But for many of us, the two or three days devoted to putting the body to its earthly rest are the easiest time of all. In our case we decided on two nights of visitation at the funeral parlor. Both my husband and I grew up in a community where viewing the body and receiving friends and family was the thing to do. My husband had been a prominent political and civic figure, with many friends, and I wanted all of them to have an opportunity to pay their respects.

For me, the very mechanics of making arrangements kept me from giving in to grief. Looking back on it now, I can also see that being the center of attention has its helpful side. Cynical as it may sound, being a new widow throws you into the role of heroine, and some of us play it in a manner which Helen Hayes might envy. It is when you retire from the center of the stage and the play goes on without you that you know real anguish.

The traditional funeral has had more than its share of criticism. Frankly, I think it is a great device to bridge the shock of death and the awfulness of bereavement which will come later.

I had always felt a little sorry for the widow besieged by large crowds at the funeral parlor, but now I found the crowds of people comforting. And there were crowds, hundreds of them both nights and all of the one afternoon. Relatives, friends, old acquaintances that we had not seen in years, political allies and foes, neighbors from our suburb and people from other cities.

The governor and his wife sent flowers, and she telephoned. The county supervisor, a group of judges, my husband's colleagues came to pay their respects. Writers and television performers, familiar faces and "names" were there. This kind of thing bolsters a family's pride and is flattering to the ego; it is a subtle tribute to the importance of the man who has died. Never again will I take lightly the responsibility to "pay one's respects." Nor will I worry too much about what to say. The numbed recipient of the attention senses and sees rather than hears.

It was not only the people of importance whose kindness was touching, but the many others—the man from the filling station, unfamiliar in his Sunday suit and white shirt, the youngsters we had taught in Sunday school, the teen-age friends of my son, inarticulate and ill at ease.

The questions were almost always the same: "Wasn't this terribly sudden? Had he been ill?" The reply became rote: "I'm sure it was more of a shock to you than it was to us. He'd been ill for some time, but he hadn't wanted anyone to know."

I stood for three hours the first evening and could have stayed on my feet all night. At the end of the evening one man who had been sitting in the back of the room came up and said, "I've been watching you comfort the mourners." Which in a sense was true.

The pageant of the parade of mourners had its human interest and its irony, too. At one point in my husband's political career he had been betrayed, I felt, by those who should have been loyal to him. It was interesting to note in the book of visitors the names of those who called during the dinner hour rather than when I was present. And as some came down the aisle I remembered how I had once imagined this very scene and had planned to say, "Yes, he's dead. Are you happy? Did you come to look and make sure?" But now my heart had no bitterness. My husband had never been a petty man. He had laughed tolerantly at my indignation—"That's politics," he had said. "You mustn't take it so seriously." Somehow the greatest tribute I could pay him was to follow his example. And so when a defector came to me, I found myself saying, "How very kind of you to come; thank you so much." And more than once the person looked away in embarrassment.

There was one man who had been a major "enemy," yet one whom my husband had come to respect and like later on. Out of the corner of my eye I spotted him, standing a little to one side and viewing my husband with a look of sadness and regret. I stretched out my hand and drew him over and expressed my appreciation for his visit. He shook his head, wordlessly, tears in his eyes.

All of this was easier for me than it was for our 15-year-old son. On the first night he asked permission to stay away to play in a scheduled concert. I granted it but insisted that he be present on the second night. I could tell it was a strain. When we got home, he blurted out some of the reasons.

"All Dad's friends keep telling me I'm the man of the house now," he said. "I don't know how to be the man of the house." And then, almost in tears, "I miss him so."

"Of course you're not a man," I said. "You're my son and a great comfort to me. And don't be ashamed to cry. Tears are good for men and women. They keep you from getting ulcers. Let the tears out."

But my eyes were still dry. I was still in shock.

Our assistant minister, the Rev. Floyd Davidson, had called to ask my suggestions for a service. He was new to our church and had known my husband only casually on the board of trustees. Though unrelated, their last names were the same, and this had been a bond. I told him a few of the things I would stress.

"Honesty, first of all," I said. "I believe everyone who knew him, friend and foe, would make mention of his complete honesty. That, and integrity. And a sense of service which led him to take jobs in political service for less money than he could have made privately."

Favorite Bible verses? Everyone should keep a list for this occasion, but I bogged down, came up with John 14.

By wonderful coincidence, at the service the minister read verse after verse which I would have wanted, the obvious ones perhaps, but the beautiful and appropriate ones, including Romans 8:38-39, my personal favorite, and many others. Moreover, in addition to the qualities I had mentioned, he added another which I had forgotten.

"There is a fourth quality," he said. "Courage. Not the flamboyant courage of the battlefield or the sinking ship but the quiet courage to meet life's problems and adversities."

I walked out of the church, proud and dry-eyed, not even sad until we descended the steps and passed through an escort of high school boys, many of whom I had known from kindergarten days. And until the limousine moved away and I saw a lawyer standing on the corner, his face twisted with grief.

The ride to the cemetery seemed unreal. The clear bright day. Snow on the ground. We did not go in the main entrance but by way of a parkway along the side which was closer to our lot. I mounted the hill, holding on to my father on one arm, my son on the other. There were a few words at the graveside, and it was over.

At home the house again was filled with people. All week I had permitted my dear friends, relatives, neighbors, to take over completely, to record messages, to list gifts, food, and flowers. We had requested that no flowers be sent, but there were 67 floral pieces at the funeral parlor and 50 at home. They were beautiful and cheering, but there were too many. I gave them to the relatives from Fulton, the relatives from Illinois, to callers—as fast as they arrived.

Some of the gestures of sympathy had been remarkable for their thoughtfulness. The teen-age daughters of friends—Julie and Mary—had cooked our dinner the second night. Friends from a journalism organization had it catered another night with sufficient servings for the out-of-town visitors.

There are many ways of paying tribute to a person who has died. We had suggested gifts to church and to several organizations, but many others were given to worthy groups and causes of all kinds. My garden club and our neighborhood improvement organization gave trees to the park in my husband's memory. Every gesture was appreciated.

Every gesture also must be acknowledged, and this is perhaps the most staggering job for the widow whose husband has had any degree of prominence. I thought how efficient and farsighted I was to begin writing the first thank-you notes as I sat under the hair dryer the day before the funeral. I scarcely envisioned the thousands I would be writing for the next six months.

Flowers are beautiful but the services of a full-time secretary offered by one friend for a day were appreciated most of all.

CHAPTER 4

Words and the Word

THE POMP AND CEREMONY WERE OVER. The out-of-town relatives had gone home. The numbness was wearing off. Still there had been no tears.

Grief should be accompanied by crying. It is wrong to bottle it up. The tears are necessary to relieve the tension and the emotional stress built up. Men as well as women, boys as well as girls must relieve the ache with honest tears. One widow, a neighbor of mine, advised by well-meaning friends to smother her tears, had a minor breakdown a few months later.

I had shed few tears in my lifetime. During adolescence there had been an occasional outburst after a disappointment or, more likely, before what the ads used to delicately term "those difficult days."

During early marriage when we had wanted children very much and none were forthcoming I had shed tears. And when my second child was expected and the doctor stood by my bedside and told me there was no way the child could live after birth, tears came. When I saw answering tears coming down his cheeks, I was shocked and remorseful. "No more tears," I said to myself sternly. "No more tears."

Four or five years later it occurred to me that I had not cried since that time, and I began to worry about it. Was some sort of trauma responsible? About this time I scratched my eye on a lilac branch. The oculist who examined my eyes said, "Did you know your tear ducts are blocked? Hadn't you noticed you couldn't cry?"

"I had noticed," I said, "but then I don't have anything to cry about."

"You're very fortunate," he said.

He opened the tear ducts and tears flowed, but not very often because in truth there was nothing or very little in our comfortable, pleasant, happy life to provoke tears, I prayed only prayers of thanksgiving.

On the first night I lay in bed, awake all night, looking at the big white pillow as if it were a mountain. On the second night a friend insisted I take a mild sleeping pill. I slept exhaustd and undisturbed but still very much on my own side of the bed.

The third night I decided sternly, "No pills. And no alcohol. I will control my body and I will go to sleep." I said to myself as I was to say many nights after that, "All you have to do now is sleep. That is the only thing you have to do. Do not think of anything else."

But early in the morning of the fourth day, the day immediately following the funeral, I awakened. Suddenly realization came to me and I began to cry, great racking, gasping sobs. Tears rushed down my face, wetting the pillows. There had always been a box of Kleenex alongside the bottle of pills on his nightstand.

"Honey," I said aloud. "Did you leave me any Kleenex?"

And, reaching blindly over to the box, I grabbed a handful, dabbed at my eyes, and then buried my head in the white mountain of his pillow and sobbed.

It was the first crying spell. It was far from the last.

Strange things make you cry. The least-expected incident.

I went to my husband's office to take home his personal effects. Dry-eyed I controlled myself as his secretary, on the verge of tears herself, showed me the stamp collection he was saving for our son and the special collection of pennies and the various bank books and savings accounts and insurance policies, some of which I hadn't known about. I was touched at all these evidences of a man who thought of his family, but I kept a tight rein on myself as a janitor brought a box and we packed away the things I was to take home.

I had left the car on the parking lot in back of his office, identifying myself to the attendant, whom I did not know. When I came out, I got in the car, drove up to his little cubicle, and called out, "How much do I owe you?"

"Oh, nothing, nothing," he said. "I couldn't charge you today. Please accept my sympathy."

I cried all the way home.

There was a sequel to this incident. The next time I had to call at the office, I decided not to park on the lot and put the man under obligation to give a poor widow perpetual parking privileges, so I looked for a place on the street. But there were no street spots and time was running short, so I was forced to go to the lot. Again as I came out I offered to pay, and again the attendant refused.

"Thank you so much," I said. "You're very kind."

"That's all right," he said and, obviously striving for the right gracious touch, added, "I just regret the entire incident."

This time I drove away, laughing with tears in my eyes. How I too regretted "the entire incident"!

Some people manage to say exactly the right thing, while others are stilted or, in an effort to be elegant, sometimes are ludicrous. Like the woman on the phone who said, "May I offer you my felicitations in your bereavement?" Many happy returns of the unhappy day!

But many were the letters—beautiful, fine, eloquent letters—which put to shame the trite platitudes which had marked my own efforts at condolences.

A blind student from our Sunday school class wrote

31

a letter in Braille. A translation was written in above the dots. The letter asked, "Is there any way in which I can be of help?" Another teen-age boy began, "I am no writer. I do not have the wit of Shakespeare nor the eloquence of Demosthenes . . . but I grieve with you at the loss of a friend. . . . When one loses a friend, one has lost part of himself." And another, a poignant letter, unsigned, read, "The entire senior high class went into a state of shock on Sunday morning. We appreciate what we have learned and wish only that we had shown our appreciation sooner."

There were many others. Official documents with seals, resolutions of regret and commendation, letters from a former secretary—"I will always remember him as a good man. . . . I never knew him to use his office for personal gain." From his barber—from the sons of friends to our son ("Everyone will miss your kind father.")

One woman, a casual acquaintance, wrote something I had begun to feel: "The City of God has a fine new citizen. Perhaps, too, you find as I do that heaven becomes more attractive all the time—so many that I have loved are peopling it. And this is, I suspect, what we mean by 'the communion of saints.'"

Because I, too, am a public figure with a newspaper following of people who feel they know me through my column, the mail was heavier than it otherwise would have been. For the first week, each morning's mail brought from 100 to 150 letters, and it took all my strength simply to open and skim them.

What to do about acknowledgments? There are several schools of thought on this. At one extreme is the woman who feels she must conscientiously send a handwritten note to everyone, even to those who only paid a courtesy call at the funeral parlor. At the other extreme is the woman who thinks, "They'll understand," and doesn't bother to acknowledge anything.

In between are the majority, more and more in recent years, for whom a printed card with a handwritten signature or perhaps a brief one-sentence note suffices.

This was not enough for me, and I began by writing notes. Notes of thanks first, for food, flowers, special favors during our time of stress. Our Saturday Night Crowd, more family than friends, was meeting at dinner the Saturday following Wednesday's funeral. I saw to it that their notes were written first, so they received them before Saturday.

But my best-laid plans bogged down badly as mail continued to come in a deluge. Finally I devised a system and for two days over that weekend operated an assembly line secretarial system from my bedroom. I read and sorted letters. One stack, the smallest, were those which had to have a personal response. A second, slightly larger, were those not really requiring any response—senders of a signed card or a routine note of thanks from an organization president or business acquaintance. These received one of the printed acknowledgment cards furnished me by the funeral parlor. Then there was the third and largest stack, those who required a response of some kind, to whom I sent a card, adding a few lines of personal comment.

As I went through the communications I wrote in addresses, copying them from the envelopes, which could then be discarded. The most welcome letters, by the way, were those with complete name, address, and zip code on the letterhead itself. But many had indecipherable scribbled return addresses which had to be checked in the telephone book. My sister-in-law Betty and three friends typed the lists of names from the letters, and three more friends addressed envelopes. Several took lists and envelopes home to address.

I then took the envelopes, signed a card and inserted it and, when necessary, wrote the accompanying note. The funeral director had furnished me with 200 cards. I returned again and again, sent some 750 within the first week, and wrote another several hundred personal notes.

All this would have been too much for a person of lesser physical stamina and was perhaps unnecessary in its scope. However, I felt that I had had the energy to write to many of these people asking for their vote and help when my husband was in politics and I could muster the same strength to give them my thanks and gratitude.

People overlook much in a widow's reactions, but those who have made a financial contribution to a church or a cause like to know that it was received and noted. These, a sizable stack of little cards which arrived each day, received top priority. And even so there were slipups. I was not notified of a gift to one organization, and the donors had to inquire of a mutual friend who tactfully told me an acknowledgment was in order, an embarrassing two months late.

Each person works differently. For me the very early morning hours are best, and I began my note writing at 5:30 a.m. At bedtime I was able to do nothing but sit up in bed and turn to the Bible or one of the many booklets of consolation sent me.

"Your book is on my bedside table," I wrote to each donor of inspirational literature, smiling a little as I thought of my bedside table with three stacks of books, each stack a foot high.

The best book was, of course, the Bible. Nightly I opened it at random, and nightly the appropriate message jumped up before my eyes.

God will give you strength, they told me. And He did.

Only Another Widow Understands

"NOBODY UNDERSTANDS BUT ANOTHER WIDOW."

This was a phrase my friend Jan was fond of using, and I was to learn its appropriateness. I thought with shame of how casual I had been in past years in my treatment of bereaved persons.

In our close-knit circle of seven couples, I was the fourth widow. All of the men had been in their 40s or 50s, and each of the other women had had grave problems of readjustment to make. Now each of them was giving to me far more than I had given them. My sympathy for them had come out of well-meaning but inexperienced ignorance. Theirs came from the depths of understanding.

Thus when I spoke to Helen of the terrible crying spells, she understood.

"I went through that too," she said, "and you know I've never been one to cry over anything. I'd bawl until my eyes were red and swollen and my nose was puffy, and then I'd look at myself in the mirror and think, 'What a fool I am! I should be glad that Paul is free from his pain and happy in heaven instead of making myself sick over him.'"

Louise was the widow who had been awakened in the middle of the night by the highway patrolman who told her that her husband had been killed on his way home from a business dinner. She understood about the pillow barrier. They had had twin beds.

"For weeks I couldn't look at Lou's empty bed," she said, "so I'd sleep in his bed and look at mine. Some-

35

how I could stand to see my bed empty, but I couldn't stand to look at his."

Jan was the most recent widow. Her husband, the gay, debonair, witty, clever life of our parties, had died six months before. I thought how only recently I had commented callously that it was high time she was "snapping out of it."

"I think Jan does everything in depth," Ginny had commented. "She's so thorough about housework and sewing and does everything meticulously. I believe she's going through grief in depth too."

There may be something in this. I plunge into things, giving myself to them completely, but I also do a job more superficially and finish it quickly. In retrospect I can see this pattern in my grief. For several months it was like a plunge into the bottom of the ocean but I believe I surfaced sooner than my friend who grieved "in depth." Thus it is futile to try to compare the experience of one woman with another or to criticize the woman who returns to her normally cheerful self. You do not know what I go through, says the Indian, until you have walked in my moccasins.

Nobody understands but another widow.

"At first you'll have that sick feeling in the pit of your stomach," Jan warned, "and the heavy feeling across your chest."

"I know," I said. "For a week I was afraid I was about to have a heart attack. They talk about 'heartache.' Now I know there literally is such a thing as an aching heart."

"It leaves you first," Jan predicted. "The sick feeling in the pit of your stomach leaves eventually too. But I'll warn you—you may have good days, even a good week, and suddenly one morning you wake up, everything is the same, it's a beautiful sunny day and there's no reason for you to be down in the dumps, and all of a sudden the bottom falls out and you're back down again."

Other books I read, books by ministers, psychologists, experts at witnessing grief, described with accuracy some of the other symptoms. Symptoms they are, because grief is as predictable an illness as diabetes or tuberculosis or cancer.

One symptom I had thought of as unique to myself until I read of it in *Ye Shall Be Comforted*, by the Rev. William F. Rogers. There may be feelings of anger or hostility, actual resentment against the person who has died, he wrote. I had expressed some of this to our very close friends at that first Saturday night gathering.

"Gary should have been happy," I said. "His funeral was the social event of the season. It combined all the elements of Christmas, the family reunion, a political rally, and our annual Open House for 200 people. I didn't mind doing all the work I always did for the parties and talking to all the people, but he used to address the Christmas cards, and it seems to me the least he could have done was to stick around and address envelopes."

This candor was expressed only to those close enough to understand. But I had to admit inner resentment, a feeling of, "Why did you go away and leave me with this mess?" A feeling, too, of "Why did you have to be so noble and long-suffering? Why didn't you tell me how bad you felt? Why didn't you wake me up that night and say, 'I'm terribly sick; call the doctor'?"

Because with the other feelings of sorrow are those of remorse and deep-seated guilt; self-accusation is a common reaction.

Why didn't I insist that he see a specialist? Why didn't I pay more attention when he was so restless that whole day?

37

Over and over I returned to two scenes which haunted me. The first—my husband standing at the doorway. "I suppose you're busy?" "Yes, TERRIBLY busy . . ." If only I could relive it. If I could rewrite the lines of that scene to make me the heroine instead of the heavy. Why hadn't I said, "No, I'm not too busy . . . what is it you want?" And what was it that he had wanted? What would the next line have been? Did he want to say, "I thought you'd like to run out to Central Hardware and look for those stair treads"? or, "There's an interesting program on television I thought you'd like to see"? Or had it been, "I'm terribly sick. Take me to the doctor"? Now I would never know.

From this scene my mind would leap to the next scene, at 7:30 a.m. that Sunday morning, the moment when a live, kind, responsive human being had twitched and jerked and turned into a "thing." Over and over I relived that moment. I read that it was helpful to relive it and to talk about it, and so I made no attempt to put it out of my mind. Gradually the memory became less painful.

At first you can think of nothing but the good side of the person who has gone. Your marriage with its customary ups and downs seems, in retrospect, like paradise. Your husband, with his human faults, is suddenly a paragon of virtue. He had no faults, or if he had, you should have excused them because he was sick.

There had been a moment a few weeks before when my husband had made a caustic remark and I had found myself glaring at him across the kitchen and thinking, "When you're dead and gone, I won't be sorry and crying the way Jan is. I'll think how *mean* you were." Now I thought back and couldn't remember why he'd been cross. Had I cooked the lima beans in insufficient water, gone off to answer the phone and let them burn?—It was a common failing of mine and one of the little things that annoyed him.

Why hadn't I tried to learn to cook the lima beans? Why hadn't I spent more time with him? Why had I been so absorbed in my own problems? Why hadn't I been kinder, sweeter, gentler?

Every widow knows this kind of breast beating, and when she asks herself, "Why wasn't I a better wife?" she must answer herself with honesty: "Because you are a human being with human frailties and human faults. He was a human being too, and had his faults."

This was consoling to me. Supposing I had been the one to die. My husband perhaps would be remembering the nightly scene when I would greet him at the door, put my arms around him and say, "I love you, honey." To which he would routinely reply, "Okay, okay, so you love me. What's for dinner?"

Thank goodness we had had the months of semi-illness, painful as they had been. I at least had some of those remarks of tenderness and gestures of consideration to remember. Once in a while I had said the right thing.

"I think I'm a much better person for having lived with you all these years," I had said only a week before. "I have much more patience and tolerance."

"I agree you're a better person," my husband had replied with amusement, "but I don't think it's from living with me. I think you would have changed with maturity anyway."

"No," I had said. "I think it's from living with you."

That exchange I clung to when that other dark moment—"I guess you're busy?" "Yes, TERRIBLY busy" —came back to haunt me.

I feel most pity for the woman to whom the shock of death comes with no warning, especially if she has been a nag or shrew or simply one of those who indifferently take a good man for granted.

But even if a widow has genuine cause for remorse and regret, she should console herself with the thought that her husband chose her, perhaps for some of the very qualities she is deploring. Unless you were a veritable virago, a devil on wheels, you may reasonably assume that your husband was attracted to your particular type of personality.

If you were slow to take hold and to insist that he have more adequate care, perhaps it is because you are a gentle, compliant woman and he liked that in a woman. If you were busy as a bee with a dozen activities, perhaps he admired and was attracted to a ball of fire rather than a dish of jelly.

I consoled myself with the thought that my husband had encouraged my activities. The very drive and involvement which led me to be making four speeches in far-flung places was also the drive which had organized 12 Sundays of "coffees" during a political campaign and supervised a platoon of doorbell ringers before a contested primary election.

"How can he stand living with her?" he had once said of another couple. "She's so stupid. She never has anything to say."

I had had plenty to say. Some of it I wish I hadn't said. It was a shame that last Saturday had not been one of the Saturdays we spent going to Central Hardware or sitting in front of the fire or working together on a project. But that was the way it had been.

You cannot berate yourself endlessly. You must accept yourself. If you were "too busy," recall that you "might have been a headache but you never were a bore." Undoubtedly your husband preferred a little migraine to a lifetime of mediocrity.

You too are a child of God. Treat yourself with the gentleness and understanding and forgiveness with which you would treat another.

CHAPTER 6

You Never Know

WIDOWS COME IN ALL SIZES, SHAPES, COLORS. All ages, too. One thing that being a widow teaches you—never assume that stranger you've just met has led a life free from grief. You simply never know.

A case in point. I was the speaker at a luncheon one day early in my widowhood. The club president was a cute and vivacious young woman, who prattled on about "Myhusband," running the two words together as wives have a way of doing.

"Aw yourhusband yourhusband," I found myself thinking. "I don't want to hear about your perfect marriage."

Perhaps she read my mind. At any rate, she said quietly, "Perhaps I feel so happy about my marriage because I know how lucky I am. And I know how you feel, too. You see, this is my second marriage. I was a widow, too."

I looked surprised. She seemed so young.

"Yes," she continued. "I was widowed when I was 23. My husband was killed when—" she mentioned a rather famous and much-publicized airplane crash. "It was the day before our second child was born."

My reaction was, "Wow." And "Whew." And, "I'd never dream . . ." You never would.

Yes, widows come in all ages and life styles. The woman who has worked most of her married life, as I had, finds it normal to return to work and getting back into the familiar routine is good therapy.

The older widow has an entirely different set of circumstances. Her children are grown and gone. Her routine has centered about only one other person—her husband—and she now may feel totally alone. She must make the decision of whether or not to go to live with children, or perhaps to move into a retirement home. Sometimes, more and more in today's world of the independent woman, she decides to "stay put," to live in her house at least for a time, until she gets her bearings.

The very young widow, in some ways, is the most vulnerable of all, the most alone of all, because she has few if any widowed friends in her age group. She may have small children who need her complete care and preclude her returning to work. Confined to the four walls of home and the company of small children, she is subject to the same cabin fever of many young homemakers but with a vital difference; there is no homecoming husband to share her burden.

Our circumstances differ but all of us have much in common, whether we are a widowed Mrs. Kennedy, the widow of a Martin Luther King, the widow of an astronaut, or the widow of an elderly gentleman known only as "Grandpop" and mourned only by a few friends and neighbors in a small town.

Our major common bond is that of loss of a part of our person—we speak of our "better half" and in some ways a husband is a "half" of ourself. And we all must adjust to life as it is, not as we would like it to be.

Often one senses that a widow has the attitude, "I'll be all right when I get over it."

But the state of widowhood is not something that you can "get over," as if it were a broken leg or a case of summer flu. You will not be "healed" or "well" or "cured." What you suffer is not a broken leg as much as it is an amputation, and you must learn a completely new approach, a new way to walk without the support you once had.

There is something else we acquire and this is the

ability to help one another. Where your snugly married friend flounders and tries to comfort you by saying, "I know how you must feel," she cannot empathize. But another widow can.

Of recent years, more and more groups have been forming among widows and widowers, who are able to help one another in practical ways and by offering emotional aid. One which has had outstanding success is THEOS (the initials stand for They Help Each Other Spiritually.) THEOS was started by an attractive young widow, Mrs. Bea Decker of Penn Hills, a suburb of Pittsburgh, Pennsylvania. An ecumenical organization, it has its headquarters at Zion Lutheran Church, 11609 Frankstown Road, Pittsburgh, Pennsylvania 15235, and its aim is to found chapters in other states throughout the land.

"Experts in the field," wrote Mrs. Becker," "say that more has been done with helping the widowed in the past five years than in the past 100 years."

There is much more that can be done. Churches in particular have scarcely scratched the surface in helping the bereaved. In a couple-oriented society, churches more than other structures, are geared to the "normal" family with few facilities for the single, the alone, the lonely.

For two years, the Missouri Conference of the United Church of Christ, has conducted an experimental retreat for the recently bereaved at its Camp Mo-Val near Union, Missouri. Asked to be a resource leader the first year, I accepted and then found myself driving to the retreat with reluctance and very little enthusiasm. What was I doing, leaving my friends and an increasingly active social life to go out and spend a weekend with a lot of little old ladies crying into their hankies?

I myself had not learned the lesson—that widows (and widowers) are all types, all ages. There were some very young ones at this retreat, some older—even a few twice widowed, and some in my own age group who have since become close friends.

The weekend was an emotional and a spiritual experience more exhilarating than any I have ever had. Over and over we found ourselves saying to each other, "I've never told this to anyone before but—" I noticed one woman crying as we sang a hymn just before my presentation so I scrapped my introduction and told impulsively how music had made me weep in those "early stages." Like the encounter groups which encourage the inhibited to open up to one another, we found it easy to drop our defenses, our masks, to be honest.

Wrote one widow when she returned home: "My sister and I cannot stop speaking of our experience and our feeling of lightness or something indescribable. We are both so terribly happy to have been a part of this program."

At the time of a death, we hear the preacher read that "All things work together for good," and we may feel bitterness, rebellion, rejection.

It may be months, even years later that we find something has worked over our tragedy and made of it something good. Widows of all ages—shapes, sizes, colors, types, life styles—may find God working within them. And the result may be that "feeling of lightness" —or "something indescribable."

CHAPTER 7

The Grisly Details

"THOSE GRISLY DETAILS."

That was the way I thought of all the business transactions any widow has to make. The papers, the forms, the documents, the applications, the transfers. This part, for me, was more difficult than the funeral, the condolences, the endless letter writing, the spells of sobbing in the middle of the night. I felt so ridiculously, inadequately, incredibly stupid.

I had been far from the traditional protected little woman who didn't know how to write a check. I had handled all the household accounts. My husband, who was thrifty by nature, had devised a simple system of budgeting whereby I spent and he saved. I paid the food, utilities, the nibbledy-buck little expenses, and spent what was left on home improvements, clothing, travel. He paid the big bills, taxes, insurance, and invested what was left. It worked very well, except that now I realized how little I knew about those all-important subjects of insurance and taxes.

For one thing, the very subject of insurance had fascinated my husband and bored me. I had mentally tuned him out when he began talking about it. How I wished I had listened. Now I realized I didn't even know how much life insurance he had had, although I was under the impression that it was very little. I had glibly assured him I "did not believe in life insurance." No amount of money would make up for his loss. Besides, we were both going to live a long time. And why did we want to leave a lot of money to our son? Let him earn his own as we had to do; he'd appreciate it more.

My husband had taken me seriously. There was very little insurance. I wished there had been more.

There were two small policies plus his GI insurance, which he had kept up. I did remember that he had once discussed the terms whereby it would be paid. The GI could elect to have his wife receive monthly payments, if she were the frivolous, improvident type, or a lump sum if she were sensible about money. He had decided I was sensible enough to be entrusted with a lump sum and suggested that I invest it at a good return.

Where does a widow begin in handling "the grisly details"? Circumstances differ, laws of various states differ and there are no precise rules which all can follow.

The best rule—and for most of those reading this book it is too late—is to sit down sensibly with your husband and prepare in advance for the time when one of you dies. Do not turn a deaf ear to the conversation which begins, "If anything happens to me . . ."

You will hear horror tales by the score, of widows whose estates were tied up in court for months while they had little or nothing to live on, widows who cannot write a check because the bank account has been "frozen," cannot go into a jointly owned safe deposit box because it has been "sealed."

When an estate of some size is involved, it is often advisable—heartless as it sounds—to go to the safe deposit box and remove its contents immediately following a death, and also to remove enough funds from a jointly held bank account to provide money for subsistence.

Even if you have had some warning and some solid preparation for your new role, another rule is paramount—consult your lawyer.

In my own case, lawyers handled everything, insurance claims, social security applications, the transfer of titles, of stock certificates, even the making of a new will for me.

Everything we owned had been owned jointly and our holdings were modest so there were no problems of an estate to go through probate court. Bank accounts were transferred to my name and the old accounts closed out. I signed papers to transfer ownership of stock. There was a charge of five dollars per document for such transfer. Numerous copies of the death certificate are necessary. My lawyer had ordered 18 and all were used.

Not all was orderly and easy, however. My friend who worked for the government made an appointment for me at the Social Security office to make application for my death benefit payment of $250 and for a monthly payment to my minor son. This was to continue to age 22 if he stayed in school. For this, various papers were required, including a marriage license.

Where was the marriage license? I vaguely recalled that we had looked at it on our 25th wedding anniversary and put it away. Where? I searched and searched, through desks, files, trunks. It never was found. Fortunately, a copy was procured at the City Hall.

Incidentally, the Social Security claim filed immediately did not bring payment for two months but then was paid retroactively.

I cannot stress strongly enough that you tell your lawyer to "follow through," to check you on every detail. He might assume that you have good sense. When you are newly widowed, you do not have good sense and often do not show good judgment.

A major error I made at this time cost me financially. My government friend gave me the name of an official to call to inquire about "other benefits which might be due" me. I called and the line was busy, so I

impatiently put it out of my mind. What "other benefits" could there be?

Three years later, driving to an out-of-town meeting
with an insurance woman friend, we talked of the financial side of being a widow. Casually she said, "Of
course, you receive your veteran's check." Oh no, I
said. "But you should," she said, "for your son—it's
just like Social Security."

I looked into it. I was eligible for $40 a month for
my son, not a large amount until you totaled it up for
a three-year period . . . $1440. It was not retroactive
but I did begin receiving it and it, too, continues until
my son is 22 or has finished his education.

My husband had his papers in good order. The folder labeled "Military" contained his discharge papers,
and one labeled "Veterans Insurance" included a tart-
ly worded letter over a typical bit of red-tape confusion; my heart ached that he should have been pro-
voked over such trivialities at a time when he was ill
and weary.

There was a folder labeled "Income Tax" and here I
found the copy of our return for the year before which
the lawyer needed. But I continued to be embarrassed
over my failure to find the marriage license.

"I can't even prove I've been married," I said.

I felt disloyal, going to my husband's bank and
withdrawing his checking account and merging it with
mine. His bank had been in the suburb where his office was located, and it was decided that it would be
best if I kept my account in the downtown bank near
me.

My checking account habitually ranged from minus
$2 to plus $200, quickly brought down each week to
minus $2 again. My husband's checking account was
in four figures. Obviously he'd been saving, perhaps to
purchase more stock, his hobby. Again I felt a pang as

I thought how thriftily he had put aside small amounts and bought stock carefully like a child in a candy store, not quite a penny's worth of this and penny's worth of that but 10 shares and 20 shares for his modest portfolio.

His goal had been a certain figure to bring in an assured monthly income to bolster our retirement annuities. I figured that if I invested my insurance benefits in stock, it would reach that figure. What irony. I temporarily deferred making any investment decisions, however, and put my one large check into a certificate of deposit.

"Do not make any big decisions immediately." This is routine advice to widows, and excellent advice. It is unwise to plan to sell a home, make new investments, make sudden changes immediately. There was no question of my selling our home, a 9-room 100-year-old house which was still home for my parents, our son, our dog and cat. In the back of my mind I decided I would stay there for six more years until our son had graduated from college and then consider a change, depending on circumstances, health, and finances.

To the woman who has prided herself on her efficiency and ability to handle all situations, it is humiliating to realize how vague and addled she is left in the aftermath of grief. I did such completely stupid things. For the first few weeks, for example, I found I forgot to plan any meals. I was constantly trying to defrost solidly frozen blocks of meat, running to the store for quick purchases. Subconsciously I was apparently thinking that there was no one for whom to cook even though there were four people. But "no one"—not a "one" who was all-important.

One insurance company delivered its check in person. I took it home—and promptly mislaid it. I found it later in a stack of discarded paper. Was this a Freudian slip—my refusal to accept money in lieu of my husband? If nothing else, it was a bad example of absentmindedness.

I found I had completely lost track of such routine household tasks as laundry and ironing. Suddenly there were no clean clothes. Fortunately my widow friend Jan spent a part of the first week with me and took over these household affairs. Help with the routine is something which most widows need in the beginning.

A new widow must not expect too much of herself. On one day during this week at home following the funeral, I made a mental list of things to do. I would return a baking dish to one friend and take one of the many lovely bowls of flowers as a thank-you for her. I would then stop by the church office to leave contributions which had been sent to me and pick up the cards which they had recording contributions made directly to the church. Then I would go to the funeral parlor and pick up some more acknowledgment cards.

The first chink in my well-laid plans was noticeable when I arrived at the home of my friend and left the flowers and then realized I had forgotten to return the baking dish which was the purpose of the visit.

On to the church, where I was completely demoralized by the look of sympathy in the eyes of the office secretaries.

"I have some things for you here," I said, reaching into my purse.

And then, idiotically, I kept coming up with check after check, of which I had absolutely no recollection.

"I don't know where these came from," I said inanely. "People must have given them to me at the funeral parlor. I sort of remember that some of them did . . ."

The girls were so kind.

"Do you have an address for this group?" they

asked, indicating one check accompanied by a long list of names.

"No,—I don't even know who any of these people are," I said.

"Maybe there was an envelope."

"Maybe. Oh, yes, here it is. Oh, yes, they're relatives of my mother-in-law."

I looked up suddenly. They were both looking at me with that pitying, sorrowing glance of sympathy. It completely undid me.

"I'll come back later," I said. "I guess I'm not very well organized yet." And, tears streaming down my face, I made a hasty exit.

I could not bring myself to go into the funeral parlor. I wanted to run home and hide. Many, many widows have told me of this urge to run to safety.

I remembered commiserating with Jan for having to go home to her big empty house.

"Oh, no," she said. "When I walk inside, I feel as if my house puts its arms around me and comforts me."

How strange, I had thought. Now, on these various forays into the world, I found myself entering the driveway with haste and a sense of relief, running into the house and having the very same sensation, as if the house were putting its arms around me and protecting me. The bedroom—which I had expected to dread because it was the scene of death—was the most cherished haven of all. There I felt safe.

On this particular day as I rushed home there was an ambulance, sirens screaming, going past the intersection. Unnerved as I was, this was the very end. I ran into the house, sobbing. Jan, who had gone out that day to have her hair done, was standing in the kitchen, tears coming down her face too.

"I just saw an ambulance," I said.

"I just saw a hearse," she said.

We clung to each other, crying and laughing at the

same time. Then we said the magic words at the same time:

"Nobody understands but another widow."

CHAPTER 8

You Can't Run Away

Don't go away to try to forget your grief. You'll only take your sorrow with you."

This, too, is excellent advice, although many well-meaning friends will advise the widow to "get away for a while, take a trip, get your mind off your troubles." A trip is good to the extent that it gets the widow away from the scene of her sorrow, gives her a rest from the endless details and the letter writing, a little respite from duties.

"I feel as if I've lived with death for months," Jan said on one occasion. "Every communication, every piece of business, every phone call is concerned with death."

Some of the experts advise the working woman to go back to work, to the daily routine. Others advocate not returning too soon. All of this is an individual matter. My decision was taken out of my hands.

For one thing, my son and I had planned a trip for his Easter vacation. The planning stage extended back almost a year. The previous spring I had attempted to get time off to attend the annual house and garden pilgrimage in Natchez, Miss., but too many commitments intervened. We talked of doing it the next year. At the same time we discussed how a quick side trip could be taken to the Mexican peninsula of Yucatan, an area in which we had long had an interest. Our son, a Spanish student, was especially eager to go there.

Two months before the scheduled time, my husband was given a promotion to the job of acting director of the Legal Aid Society. He hoped the promotion would be a permanent appointment, but this meant he could not take any time off during this crucial period.

"You go ahead and go without me," he urged us. "I'll stay home and look after my job and Grandma and Grandpa and the house."

We demurred—but we really wanted to go. Finally we decided we would go away, but just for 10 days and would take a longer family vacation in summer. Our reservations were made and paid for by a deadline, March 1. Then on March 5 our world fell apart.

"I guess we won't take our trip," our son said on the way back from the hospital.

"Let's wait and see. I can't think now."

Friends urged us to go, to "get away from it all." When the deluge of phone calls, letters, flowers descended on me, I found myself feeling the desperate need to "get away from it all." Would anyone criticize us for taking a pleasure trip so soon? Well, let them.

The Natchez part of the trip had been planned with another couple who were taking their car, a delightfully gay and thoughtful pair, and the three days in Natchez was a restful time.

I had returned to the office for one week before I left, to sort through more stacks of mail and to write one column. My column is a personal one and usually is accompanied by a smiling picture of the author. Both I and my editors were disturbed as to how I could continue. Somehow I had to write about my loss; most readers would know (it seemed to me that most of them had written), but I could not simply return with a flip, bright column of the type I usually wrote. And the smiling picture would be unthinkable.

The simplest solutions are always the best. I wrote about my husband's death, as dispassionately and factually as I could, and concluded with a mention of the vacation trip we would be taking. We would be celebrating Easter away from home, I wrote:

"Celebrating? Yes, because even the sad and sorrowful, perhaps especially the sad and sorrowful, have cause for joy at Easter. 'Because I live, ye shall live also.'

"My husband believed this without doubt or question. And so do I."

The column in its honesty apparently struck a responsive chord. I was to hear from many, many readers and especially from many widows, a touching number of whom had known the same bereavement the same week.

The picture used with the column was not a smiling one. It was a picture which my friends were to refer to as "that sad widow picture of yours." It was made at a studio in Natchez by a talented portrait photographer who used expert lighting, psychology, and even wired music to come up with what we hoped would be a somewhat spiritual expression, serious but soulful, not doleful. She did her best, but it was still a "sad widow picture."

No lover of old houses and beautiful gardens could be completely sad in Natchez at Pilgrimage time. A friend, Mrs. Hazel Knapp, is a hostess at Arlington, one of the handsome homes. She gave us a personally conducted tour, and we were overcome with Southern hospitality.

One night we attended the pageant with its costumed beaux and belles and ante bellum setting. It reminded me, I told my companion Jane, of the scene in *Gone with the Wind* in which Scarlett O'Hara, a new widow, is prevailed upon to dance with Rhett Butler and scandalizes staid Atlanta. A few minutes later I was to be more forcibly reminded.

"In the Cotillion number," Hazel told us, "the couples separate, and the young ladies come to the sidelines and get men to dance with. So let's sit George on the end . . ."

"Oh, no, you don't," said George. "I'm not getting up there."

But we sat him on the end. The couples separated. A young lady headed straight for him, and we all laughed.

I was still laughing when I looked up and saw a young man in uniform bowing in front of me.

"Get up," Hazel ordered, pushing me. "Here, I'll hold your coat."

And before I knew what I was doing I was waltzing around the dance floor, I a widow of only two weeks. Shades of Scarlett O'Hara! Worse than that, I was enjoying it.

"Hazel," I whispered when I sat down, "there are St. Louis people here. Several of them recognized me on the tour today, and some offered condolences. What will they ever think?"

"They'll think you're entering into the spirit of the Pilgrimage as you should when you're a guest," said Hazel serenely.

From Natchez my son and I flew to New Orleans, where we met my Aunt Margaret and her niece whom I have always called Cousin Margaret. I remembered how shattered Aunt Margaret had been when my Uncle Albert had died of a heart attack. That had been 17 years ago. I had not seen her since.

She was tinier and older than I remembered her, but spunky and gay and good company.

"When are you coming to St. Louis?" I asked as we parted. "We used to have such fun when you two visited us."

Her chin quivered, her lip quavered. "I'll never come to St. Louis again," she began. And the tears rolled down her cheeks.

Oh, dear, I thought. Seventeen years later. Oh, dear. Do you never recover?

That afternoon we flew on to Merida in Yucatan,

and from there a guide took us by car to Chichen Itza, and a luxurious oasis in the middle of the jungle. We stayed in a thatched hut and slept under a mosquito-netting canopy and swam in a pool in which purple bougainvillea floated. An ideal place to "get away from it all."

The hour of 5:30 was still a low point in the day for me, the time when we had had our before-dinner talks. On the first night at Chichen Itza at 5:30 I seated myself at a table on the patio just outside the bar and ordered a Margarita. The man at the next table smiled, leaned over and introduced himself. He was from a neighboring suburb in our county. I introduced myself and explained my circumstances and my widowhood. Soon his wife came along and introductions and explanations were again in order.

"Oh, yes," she said. "I remember reading about it. It was very recent, wasn't it?"

It was indeed, and although her manner was kindness itself, I realized that it had been too recent. I didn't belong there in that gay vacation setting. I was like a ghost at the feast.

The trip is hazy in my mind. The visits to the ruins, the day and night in Merida, the markets, the dining room where a trio played Cole Porter music, the flight to the island of Cozumel, a jewel of an island with the clearest blue-green water I have ever seen, the sandy beach, the surf, the sun, the sky.

And the happy family groups. The children crying, "Daddy—oh, Daddy!" The mothers saying, "Ask your father." The couple on the beach who kissed and cuddled for three days. On the fourth day he came out alone, lay on his beach towel, and began to read Truman Capote's *In Cold Blood*. Was the honeymoon over or was the bride sunburned? I never knew.

My teen-ager appeared to be enjoying himself, although from time to time he would look at me anxiously.

"You're all right now," he'd say. "You're over it, aren't you?"

"Oh, yes," I'd lie. "I'm fine. I'm over it."

One night I must have snored or snorted and he must have remembered that I described the death rattle as something like a snoring noise. At any rate, he was by my bed in a flash.

"Are you all right?"

"Yes," I said sleepily. "I'm fine. Go back to bed."

In the morning he asked, "Do women snore?"

"We deny it," I said, "but your father always told me I did."

It brought up a point widows must remember. A child, even an almost grown child, who has lost one parent is unduly anxious about the health of the remaining parent. I soon learned never to make my usual remarks, "I'm half dead today," "I feel awful," "Don't know if I'll make it or not," etc. Instead I affected a smiling, bouncy manner and emphasized my exuberant good health and vitality. Later on when I had an insurance examination, a medical checkup, I was careful to remark on how healthy the doctor said I was and how well I felt. By summer his anxiety over my health seemed to have disappeared.

But no matter how much I reassured him on the trip, I was far from "over it."

Part of it was the feeling of loneliness at being far away from home. In our bedroom I had sensed my husband's presence, a continuity of life which was lost in the tropical setting. Also my spiritual life had gone down from its early exalted state.

I believed—and still believe—in personal immortality. I believed—and still believe—that we should not grieve for the dead. I have had little personal experience with the beyond but I had experienced one brief incident which had strengthened my convictions.

It had happened the night that Jan's husband, our close friend Charles, had died. I had been with them at the hospital; it was also a rainy, gloomy Sunday.

That evening at home I had tried to watch a much-publicized movie on television. But my mind kept wandering to our dying friend, and I found myself praying earnestly, then frantically.

"O Lord, please make a miracle. Let him live. Take a year from my life and give him one more year."

I found myself longing for bedtime when I could lie still and continue my prayers alone. Yet suddenly, sometime between the end of the movie at 10:15 and our 10:30 bedtime, I felt a surge of happiness, a peaceful, serene feeling; I could almost sense the message, "You don't have to pray anymore." For one wild moment I thought my prayers had been answered. Then reality assured me this could not be. In the morning I found he had died—at 10:20 p.m.

After my husband's death I found myself waiting for some feeling akin to this sense of peace and reconciliation, but it was not forthcoming. Jan had told me that she thought she had seen Charles leaning over her on Christmas night—looking young and happy as he had looked years ago.

Perhaps it would happen to me, I thought. Perhaps on Easter Sunday. What more appropriate time?

But Easter came and went, and there was nothing. I attended services in the pretty little Catholic church in Santa Maria. The priest welcomed the visitors in English. It was very nice. But spiritually I was in a vacuum. Or rather I was standing at a wall, unable to find a door to get through. A blank wall. My husband was gone. He had vanished through the wall. I was shut out.

Easter Monday, the day we left for home, was an

all-time low. I arose at 5 in the morning, walked up the beach, far far up the deserted sandy strip, and threw myself down on the sand and wept. Then I wrote in the sand, "Gary, I love you" and watched until the waves crested and broke and swirled up and washed it all away.

You can get away, but you cannot "get away from it all." You take it all with you. Jan learned this on a trip to Nassau early in her bereavement. Many another traveling sorrowing widow has found out the same thing.

It reminded me of a college quip: "I tried to drown my troubles, but I found out they could swim."

My troubles refused to be drowned in the beautiful green-blue waters of the Caribbean. When I returned home, they were still there. And so were six fresh bouquets of flowers and 150 more letters of condolence.

CHAPTER 9

Pulled Together—Pulled Apart

IT WAS THE END OF THE FIFTH WEEK. Approximately the time when I had started saying of Jan, "Surely she ought to be pulling herself together by now. After all, it's been five weeks . . ."

And here I was, not pulled together. Still pulled apart more often than not.

There were more of "the grisly details." The business of selling my husband's car was among them.

We had almost identical cars, gray Volkswagens—"His and Hers" we called them. His was older but had been driven less and was in much better condition than Hers.

The car had become a symbol during the months that he had been ill. Every night I would walk the dog at 5:15. Usually at 5:20 or 5:25 the car would pull into the driveway and I would say a little prayer inside me —"Thank You, God, for bringing him home safely again." Then I would race Spot to the car and greet my husband with an effusive, "Why it's Daddy. Here comes Daddy." And invariably he would say something like, "Are you walking that silly dog again?" or, "Don't give me that Daddy business." And we would go inside and I would say, "I love you," and he would say, "Never mind—what's for dinner?" A typical family exchange.

Now at 5:15 I would walk Spot and return him to his pen and 5:30 would find me standing at the door, eyes strained toward my husband's car parked in the driveway where it had been all day. I would find myself pretending it had just arrived and he would be getting out.

"Please God," I would pray. "Let me see him. Just for a second, sitting at the wheel of the car. Smiling at me. Happy and relaxed. Just for one second." My eyes would strain, but the car would remain empty.

While we were on our Easter vacation, I had asked our regular repair man to take the cars in to his garage and provide any necessary services and advise me which one to sell. He said that both were in good condition but perhaps it was best to sell the older one and keep the newer for a better trade-in when I decided to buy again.

I decided I would sell it quickly. A neighbor had told me of a woman she knew whose husband had bought a $5,000 car a few days before his death. His wife had kept the car in the garage for 20 years. It's "His Car," she said. "I can't part with it." I could not afford that kind of sentimentality even though my investment was only one fifth as great.

"Keep it for your son," some advised. "He'll be 16 in October." But that was six months away, and the car would depreciate undriven. A certificate of deposit for the same amount of money would pay interest.

Then the situation was quickly taken out of my hands. A friend mentioned to another friend that I had a car to sell. A nice young couple came to look at the car, liked it, and said they would buy it. After three days of frantic search for the title to the car—"What's the matter with me, can't I find anything?" I thought in desperation—it showed up, jammed behind a desk drawer.

The car was sold. The nice young couple drove it down the driveway, and I watched it disappear and then took care of practical matters, buying the certificate of deposit and calling the automobile insurance man to cancel the insurance on the car I had sold.

There was a refund forthcoming, which was gratefully received. It had all worked out very well, but it had been a greater emotional strain than I had imagined.

It is interesting to note which items are easier to part with. With one woman, a man's clothes are so much a part of him that she cannot bear to give them away. Others clean out the closet with one fell swoop.

Clothing had never been an important part of my husband's life. He had dressed with meticulous neatness. His shoes had always been shined, his collars impeccable; there was never a spot on his necktie. I found myself eyeing other men critically and finding them sorely wanting. But still the clothes themselves were not important.

I would advise the widow with a large stock of good —often unworn—clothing to advertise in the classified columns and then turn the sale over to a friend and leave the house on the day it is conducted. In my case there was not that great a supply. I found a friend who wore shoes of the right size and was happy to have them. My father knew of a bus driver who was approximately the same suit size. He came over one evening, tried on a suit, and took the contents of the closet. Old clothing I gave to a rummage sale. A few choice pieces, several expensive woolen shirts and a bathrobe, I kept for our son. There was no sentimentality involved for me—although it was hard to discard the paint-spattered work shoes.

A widow friend had a much more difficult time. She finally disposed of most of her husband's extensive wardrobe and then began having nightmares about it.

"I dream that he has come back wearing only a dressing gown and finds I've given all his clothes away," she said.

Each widow has her own special stumbling block, the time of day that is loneliest—for me, 5:30, for another friend the end of the day when men were coming home from work, for Jan the early morning hours when she would take a cup of coffee in to her husband in the bedroom. For each widow there is the routine action that was performed so often as teamwork that it is dreadful done alone.

For me the most difficult single moment was the first Saturday morning that I went to the supermarket alone. It had been such an established pattern—driving over the suburban streets, parking at a certain spot on the lot, taking up our customary roles, as stylized as a Japanese play. "Do you have the empties?" "Yes, do you have the coupons?" Then walking into the store, separating as he recovered the deposits on the empties and I disengaged a cart, then reuniting at the bacon counter. That first day I took my son with me, but this brave sight of widow and tall boy and the sympathetic glances it aroused was worse than going it alone.

Watching the same television programs was next to impossible, even the ritual of 10 o'clock news had its memories. Its silly husband-wife jokes.

"Are you going to the bathroom on Weather?" he would ask.

"No, you go on Weather. I'll go on Sports."

For the past year I had tried to keep him company as he spent more and more time in a sedentary way before the television set at night, but I disliked blood and thunder and thrillers.

"How can you watch that stuff? It makes me nervous," I would say.

But there had been two or three shows we had watched with mutual enjoyment—Danny Kaye, Dean Martin, Andy Williams. I found I couldn't bear to watch any of these. I did not turn on the television set until the fifth or sixth week, when my father said, "Frank Sinatra is on an hour show—it's about half over. Don't you want to watch it?"

"Thanks," I said. "I'll turn it on."

I walked in the bedroom, flipped the switch in time to hear: "When you're alone—who cares for starlit skies . . ."

It was so appropriately lugubrious that I laughed instead of crying.

Tears came most often, I found to my surprise, when I was driving the car. On Friday afternoon at the end of the fifth week I was driving from the city on the express highway. I had been to a Church Federation luncheon and listened to the reports of the chaplains at hospitals and institutions. They had had many sad stories, and I had tried to feel sympathetic toward the poor soul playing solitaire in the chronic hospital. But I did not have enough pity to spare.

I thought of Jan, who had told me that her sister-in-law, in order to "get her mind off her troubles," had regaled her with tales of people who were "much worse off," children suffering napalm burns in Vietnam, couples who had lost their only child, and so on. Finally, in rebellion, Jan had burst out:

"Naomi, I'm not interested in anyone else's misery. I'm only interested in my own misery."

I, too, was only interested in my own misery.

I was on my way to interview a woman, an old friend who had written a book on flower arranging. She was a courageous person, confined to a wheelchair for some years, but you never thought of her as being confined, because her spirit was so free. She was as gay and lighthearted as if trouble had never touched her. But it had. Her only child, a daughter, had married a young man during World War II, and he had been killed a few months later on a landing in the Pacific. The daughter had never remarried, and she always seemed to me as fresh and girlish and untouched as if she were still a bride of 22 instead of an office secretary of 44.

Again a part of me sorrowed for the friend who

would never know what it was like to hold her grand-children. And yet . . .

My own miseries intervened. I suddenly found my-self crying with greater intensity than I had yet done. Crying and railing against God and man.

"God, why did You do this to me? I deserved better than this. I'm not perfect, but I've tried . . . and he tried. He was so good, such a fine, good person. If You had to punish us, why didn't You punish me and strike me dead? He was worth 10 of me.

"And Jesus, You promised: 'I will not leave you comfortless,' but You have. I am comfortless. Oh, I'm comforted all right—by friends and letters and flow-ers. By words, words, words. What comfort are words?"

In my ridiculous fury, I lashed out at my dead hus-band.

"And you," I addressed him. "You've been gone five weeks and you haven't once made yourself felt to me. Where is your spirit that is supposed to stay on? Where is the love of those who have gone on that peo-ple tell me is all around us? You've left me, you've left me . . . and you're never coming back."

And the weight, the heavy weight across my heart tightened and pressed and strangled.

"O God, O God, how long, how long? Why hast Thou forsaken me? Why can't I open my heart? Why is it closed, closed, closed? Why can't I feel my hus-band is alive instead of dead? In the cold tomb."

I tell all of this baldly, nakedly, because there must be many other women who have suffered the same thing in secret.

It was Saturday morning, the end of the fifth week. Again the ordeal by supermarket and again the kind faces and the strangers who stopped me: "I haven't had the chance to express my sympathy, but I want you to know . . ."

People mean so well, but I tended to agree with my son, who had said, "If one more person extends me his sympathy, I'm going to extend it right back."

There were two attractive young women working at the bakery counter.

"Aren't you the writer? I thought you were. I wanted to tell you how much I appreciated that Easter column," said one of them. She nodded toward her companion clerk, "We've gone through it, both of us. We know what it's like."

There they were, two young women, so young, so attractive. And widows. I managed a wan smile.

"Someone ought to tell women how horrible it is," I said. "You just don't know what it's like until you've experienced it."

"I know." The young woman's face was kind and sober. "But you couldn't tell anyone in advance. You have to go through it to know."

The woman at the cash register spoke to me.

"I want to tell you how much I appreciated your column at Easter. I'm a widow too, you know, and I think it's wonderful that you brought in that part about the spirit . . . that life goes on."

"Thank you," I said. "Thank you very much."

I sat in the car a few minutes, thinking with shame of my own doubts and distress. How could you give hope to others when you had so little yourself? I watched people coming through the automatic swinging doors. How many women there were, older women alone, pushing carts. Widows, I supposed. I had never thought of it before; I had never really noticed them. But there they were.

In my mind's eye it seemed as if I could see an endless parade of lonely women walking by themselves. Widows.

CHAPTER 10

Beautiful Spring

"YOU'RE LUCKY TO BE GOING THROUGH THIS IN SPRING," another widow said to me. "I had to endure these early stages in the bleak, cold months of winter, and it was much worse."

Well, maybe. But it is my impression that the first month or two of agony is just that, no matter what the season. There were times when I found myself thinking of the lines by Edna St. Vincent Millay: "It is not enough that yearly down this hill, Spring comes, babbling like an idiot and strewing flowers."

It even seemed to me that misery would be more appropriate to a stark, black-and-white world than to this happy, colorful time of year. The fragrance of lilacs, the drifts of blue woods phlox brought back memories of college days, the lilacs along the campus walks, the Sundays we'd hike into the woods and come back, arms laden with the blue phlox. The time I had leaned out the dormer window of the dormitory, holding my bouquet, and he had stood below to take a picture. The faded little snapshot is in an album somewhere. And ever since then, blue phlox has meant that special Sunday. I have it planted throughout the woodland of our yard.

"There has never been a spring like this," people were saying. It was prematurely warm, and everything was blooming ahead of schedule. The late April red-and-yellow striped tulips bloomed in late March, the lilacs in early April instead of on the last day, the May iris a few weeks later. The dogwood showered its white bouquets along the street. We had planted one, in a neighborhood improvement drive a few years before, and this year it was glorious.

Two friends, Elva and Ike, came over and planted a flowering crab tree as a memorial, near the patio of our backyard.

"We've had such good times on this patio," Elva said. "You've had such wonderful big parties—and you will again."

The tree had pink-lavender blossoms. Nearby was a lavender azalea surrounded by blue phlox. In the perennial border, pink and white tulips and white arabis were in bloom—and more blue phlox. It was a beautiful picture.

People have imaginative and thoughtful ideas. Dottie B. gave me a check for the garden, she said, for anything that I would like. I decided on a statue to put in a quiet corner of the woods, a place where I had always gone to sit and meditate. There was a stone bench there and a redbud tree.

Selecting the right statue took a lot of deciding. Not a St. Francis, not a Kwan Yin, not anything I saw at first glance in the courtyard of statuary where I shopped.

The single-figure statues looked lonely, the boy with a shell, the girl looking up at the sky. I'll be lonely enough when I sit there, I thought. I don't want something to make me lonelier. Then I saw the two figures, a boy and a girl, the boy quiet and steady-eyed and calm-looking, the girl leaning to one side, restlessly gazing at some far horizon. "Playmates" was the name of the statue. Two babes in the woods, as we had been as college youngsters, walking along Hinkson Creek, picking the blue phlox and stopping to be twined in one another's arms . . . as the sun shone and the birds sang.

I put the little figures under the rosebud tree. The tree appeared to be half dead this year—symbolic? It might have to be removed, but I decided to let it stay temporarily. If it were replaced, a pink dogwood might go well. . . . The gardner is always planning a garden even in times of grief.

For the time being, I planted flower seeds, some blue asters, a few stray plants of blue phlox, some pink oxalis, and a pink rose tree of China at the foot of the redbud. Along the path of pine needles leading to the quiet corner, the azaleas were in bloom, first a white one, then a dark pink, then a light pink, then a lavender.

Walking back to the house from the woods, I noticed something at the foot of another tree. The ostrich fern, a dead lump of nothing planted a month ago.

It was stretching up a curled finger of soft, feathery green. And suddenly the terrible weight lifted from my heart.

CHAPTER 11

Good Days and Bad

THERE USED TO BE A POPULAR SONG THAT WENT, "It's so nice to have a man around the house." It is so true.

"You ought to form an organization like A.A.," my widow friend Jan said to me. "A group that would counsel new widows and help them do things. For instance, I didn't know anything about some of the mechanical things around the house. I didn't even know how to turn on the furnace. I had to lie on my stomach with a lighted paper to reach the pilot, and I was scared to death I'd blow the house up."

As efficient as I thought I was, there were many household details of which I was ignorant. Fortunately we have a fine carpenter who has done a great many home improvements in our old house. He had been asked to give us an estimate on a new front porch the week before my husband's death. He came to see me a short time after the funeral, and after some brief inner debate I decided to go ahead and have the major improvement made.

"I think Gary would have wanted me to do it, don't you?" I asked his secretary for reassurance.

She started to laugh. "Do you know what he said about that porch?"

"No, what?"

He said, "I'm going to stall her on it as long as I can."

I laughed too. "Well, he has," I said.

I went ahead with the new porch. Such decisions were now mine to make, the responsibility and expense mine too.

But having Bob, the carpenter, at work that spring was a real boon.

"I'm going to see to it that all your door locks are in good condition," he said. "I want you to be safe. Can either Grandpa or Bruce use a gun?"

"Ooh, no," I shuddered. "I wouldn't have a gun."

But we do have good locks now. And it was Bob who fixed the upstairs windows and cleaned the gutters and cleared the old screens and storm sash from the basement. My Uncle John, also a handy man around the house, put new steps in one room and advised me on painting.

Every widow needs men friends like this. One often hears the familiar complaint of wives that an attractive widowed neighbor is constantly asking their husbands to help put a washer in a faucet or nail a board. The wives hint that the widows are poaching on their preserves, trying to get their man away.

Wives can rest at ease. Few fresh new widows want another woman's husband.

"I want a husband," one woman wrote to me, "but not the husband of any other woman. I want my own husband back."

If other women only realized it, most widows look with distaste on other men. Jan and I compared notes on this.

"Charles was so particular about his appearance," she said. "His trousers had to hang just so, his shoes were polished. Now I look at other men on the street and in elevators and think how sloppy they look. I never see one I'd give a second glance."

I found this to be true and at times was almost violent about it. Looking at a group of men walking down the street, I would feel, "Why are they alive when my nice husband is dead? Lord, I'll make a trade. I'll trade all three of those men, I'll trade every man on this street if You'll bring mine back. He was worth more than all of them."

The new widow idolizes and feels adulation for her departed mate. He had no flaws. He was kind and good and true and patient and loving and gentle and generous and noble. And besides all that, he knew how to turn on the pilot light of the furnace and how to put a washer in the leaky faucet and what to do when the dishwasher made that funny noise.

It was a Saturday at the end of the seventh week. It was one of those bad days. Bobby Kennedy, asked about Jacqueline Kennedy in the early stage of her widowhood, had replied, "Well, she has her good days and her bad days." I was having one of my bad days.

"You go along just fine," Jan had predicted. "A whole week goes by and you're gay and sunny and you think, 'Oh, great, I'm over it.' The tight feeling across your chest, the weight, the sickness disappears. Then one morning you wake up and nothing is any different, the weather is fine, it's a beautiful day, you're the same person, but the bottom has dropped out and you're down in the dumps, lower than ever."

It was so true. The bottom had dropped out on that Saturday and I had the screaming meemies. But still there was work to be done.

We were redoing the guest room. Uncle John was patching the plaster, and I went to the hardware store to get the paint. It was not the best place for a lonely widow, a hardware store. All the man talk. All the old familiar sights and sounds. The kindness in the eyes of the proprietor. He had known my husband in World War II days.

"Where are you parked? I'll help you carry that paint."

The act of kindness caused tears to spill over. I cried all the way home. O God. O God. O GAWD!

Uncle John had advised a coat of aluminum paint

over the dark wood paneling which I hoped to change to a light apple green. I busied myself with the base coat. Soon Saturday was over.

Sunday morning. It was raining. Not another rainy Sunday! It had been a beautiful spring, but it had rained at some time during every Sunday since that fateful March 5.

From 7 a.m. to 9 a.m. I painted. Then, suddenly, looking out the window at the blue phlox, the phlox we had gathered in our college days, I couldn't stand it. I had to go to the cemetery and take a bouquet of blue phlox. First I would go there and then back to church in time for the 11 o'clock service.

In the kitchen I picked up a small jar, a maraschino cherry jar left over from those winter cocktails. I filled it with water, picked a handful of phlox in the rain-soaked garden, and put them in the jar and started out.

It was the first time I had been to the cemetery since the funeral. We were not much on cemetery visiting in our family. We decried such practices as that of a man we knew whose wife had died tragically, a suicide. He had been spending every Sunday at her grave, a thermos of coffee and a sandwich to keep him going.

At the other extreme, we had never visited the grave of my husband's father, although we had both adored him. My husband considered it a futile practice. The soul isn't there, he used to say. Why go and stand and cry? It's only the earthly shell.

But I had to go. And this time I would drive to the main entrance rather than the parkway approach so I could go past the quaint Victorian building and skirt the edge of the lake.

Of course I got lost. And annoying and frustrating as it was, I had to laugh at myself.

"This is the final straw," I thought. "I've misplaced everything—marriage license, car title, income tax, insurance check. Now I've lost my husband. I don't even know where the body is buried."

I found myself stifling an impulse to call out, "Where are you? Honey—where are you?"

Instead I retraced my way to the other entrance at the parkway side. "Now how did the funeral procession go? It was up a hill . . . I know it was on a hill . . . I walked up, holding on to my father and my son."

I got out of the car at the bottom of a hill and walked up over the soggy turf. At the crest of the hill I saw two small headstones. They were marked for my Uncle Leonard and my Aunt Lily, brother and sister of my Aunt Olie who, with Uncle John, owned the lot. Then that new mound must be—only there were two new mounds. For one crazy moment I thought, "I'm dead too. They've buried me alongside him." But then I realized one bare place must be from the earth that had lain there and the other would be the grave. Only which was which?

Suddenly, standing there, another voice spoke within me. "How ridiculous!" it said. "It doesn't matter which is the grave because he isn't there."

My heart refused to honor the doubts of my intellect. He was simply not there. I knew it. I put the flowers down roughly in the center of the plot for all of them, Uncle Len, Aunt Lil, and him, and started down the hill.

Just then the sun came out. And as I drove away the words came to my mind: "He is not here. . . . I am the Resurrection and the Life. Though he were dead, yet shall he live . . ."

"This is the end of another chapter," I thought, "the chapter of grief and doubt." It wasn't quite, of course. The battle went on, between faith and doubt, between hope and despair. But in a way I had turned a slight curve in the long path. And thus the eighth week began.

CHAPTER 12

To Bank and to Market

THERE IS A PERIOD WHEN EACH MORNING YOU FACE IT AFRESH. Then comes the time when you must face the fact that it is always going to be that way. And this is the hardest time of all."

An older friend, Adele, a widow for many years, told me this one day as she and another woman were taking me to lunch—one of the many kind morale-boosting gestures of my numerous friends. It was very true.

In the beginning I found myself resisting the blunt fact of death. Irrational as I knew it to be, I found myself thinking, "When he gets back."

We cleaned the basement and his workbench, which had been in a snarl of confusion for a long time. We had new draperies made for the living room and a sofa reupholstered and the new porch built. Many of these projects had been in abeyance during his illness. Looking back, it seemed to me that every time I had mentioned a home improvement or a change, it had been met with the gentle but firm: "Do we have to do that now?" My temperament is of the kind which says, "Do it now," whether it's a pleasant or unpleasant chore.

The improvements made a difference in our surroundings, a pleasant, uplifting difference. I recommend a redecorating project for any widow in the doldrums. Fresh colors, clean rooms, even a modest expenditure of money are a tonic for a woman.

But, ridiculously, I found myself thinking, "Won't he be pleased? Won't he be surprised when he comes back and sees . . ." and then the shock would hit me afresh that he was not away on a trip; he was dead.

On one occasion I even went so far as to start clipping from the front page of the newspaper a story about an old acquaintance of my husband's who was being mentioned for a high political office.

"He'll be so interested to read this when he . . ."

Before my mind could finish the sentence, the awful truth dawned anew, and I crumpled the paper and threw it into the wastebasket and leaned my head down on my typewriter for a moment until the shaking and the dizziness passed away.

I still received letters by the dozens, more after the column telling of my husband's death than in the month immediately after it had happened. And the sorrow and desolation of some of them struck me as forcibly as my own sorrow.

"I put on a brave face all day at my job," wrote a woman who had been widowed much longer. "Why these tears that won't stop when I'm alone? Am I displeasing God?"

An elderly man wrote me of his 56 years of happy marriage and sent me the sympathies of him and his wife. I wrote an acknowledgment—more and more of these were being dictated to a secretary or answered with a form letter and a brief sentence of personal reaction. In it I said, "I hope you have many more happy years together." By return mail I received a letter from him. His wife had read my letter and had walked out into the backyard—and died instantly of a heart attack. Now it was my turn to console him.

Some, many in fact, had a beautiful Christian approach to their bereavement.

"I am a Christian and know that when God speaks His will, it is to be done; but I'm also human," wrote one woman, "and I said to my Master, 'Why?' even as Christ on the cross asked, 'Why have I been forsaken?'

78

Loud and clear came the answer, 'I gave you your husband for 36 happy years. Now he is with Me safe and happy. You have time to serve Me only.'

"I enlisted in the Christian Service Corps and will serve as teacher and counselor in state youth camps and vacation Bible schools.

"Remember," her letter concluded, "if we had no tears, there could be no rainbows. God did not promise us a life without burdens; that comes to us in the next world."

This woman's reaction, to dedicate her life to humanity, is perhaps the best answer of all to grief. As I analyzed the sorrow of other widows, it seemed to me it was longest-lasting among those who had little or no creative or humanitarian outlet. Not that I would blame anyone for not being a "do-gooder." The impulse to serve is not equally distributed among us. There are those for whom the endless busy-work of volunteer groups is a bore rather than a satisfaction. Certainly there is little to be gained from simply "keeping busy." But there is much to be gained from thinking of others rather than yourself.

In my own case, a church retreat and planning session in May was good for my spirits, held, as it was, in a lovely country setting among the good-natured good people I had known for many years at our church. Worshiping together, walking around the lake in quiet companionship was like a long cool drink quenching my thirst for something other than the mundane and material things of life.

A widow in our church had just announced that she and our widower assistant minister would be married, and this was cause for rejoicing and much teasing.

"We widows are so happy when one of us snares one of you widowers," I told him. "We outnumber you, you know."

"I know," he replied. "I read an article the other day

which said that widows outnumber widowers four to one. I told Peg that the Bible tells us to take care of the widows and she has a big house. It seems only fair that I should take care of my share. But do you know, she wasn't a bit interested?"

"That's the trouble with successful widows," I said. "They're selfish. They won't share the wealth."

But one widow is happy when another finds happiness. It was the familiar saying which Jan and I had adopted: "No one understands but another widow." As I attended luncheons to make my scheduled spring speeches—for I had returned to the routine after Easter—I found more and more women greeting me with a warm handshake and the words, "I know what you're going through. I'm a widow too." And there would pass between us a glance, a kind of secret look of understanding which said, "Ah, yes, you know." Sometimes the woman was very old. Sometimes, as was the case at a gay cocktail party, she was young and lovely. But the look down deep in her eyes was the same.

And it must be the same for any widow, no matter what hers or her husband's position in life. Whether your husband was a Franklin Delano Roosevelt, struck down by a stroke as he sat for his portrait, or a John Fitzgerald Kennedy, felled by an assassin's bullet as he rode through the streets of Dallas, or a lesser politician of local renown with many friends and a following in his town, or a quiet little old man in a nursing home, or a farmer or a day laborer known only to a tiny circle of family and neighbors, his death leaves a gaping loss. Each woman feels the sense of losing a life's companion, the person to whom you were married. In many ways, the flesh is indeed "made one." When the other person is ripped away, a part of your body is torn from you. There is a wound. I was to feel at times as if I had been rudely cut down the middle by a buzz saw. Only half of me was left.

My widow friend Jan and I were together often.

"You shouldn't spend so much time together," some people said. "You're not good for each other."

But we thought we were good for each other in therapeutic ways. One evening we sat and talked for five hours, and our subject of conversation was our husbands. We were amazed to find it was 1 a.m.

"Thank goodness we didn't bore our friends," we giggled.

Part of her sorrow and mine, too, was the fact that our husbands were in the prime of life. Both had much to give professionally and personally. In both cases we had looked forward to retirement, to a slowing down of our hectic though happy pace of life.

"I could see Charles and myself sitting by the fire and enjoying each other's companionship," she would say. "Now we've been robbed of our old age together."

"I had looked forward to our retiring and being at home more," I would say. "All these years while I've scrambled to keep things going, I've said, 'Just be patient—in a few years the grandparents will be gone and our son will be in college and we'll be alone and life will be more orderly.' I had visions of dinner by candlelight with lobster thermidor instead of Bonnie buttered steaks and canned spaghetti. I used the chipped everyday dishes, but I used to think I'd use the good china and silver someday. Now the someday will never come."

The morning after our late night talk we went to church, I to teach my Sunday school class and Jan to regular services. In the midst of the services, a woman in the congregation had what appeared to be a stroke. Her husband and another man helped carry her out. They held her upright, but her little feet were dragging the floor. After church Jan told me that she had been sitting directly across the aisle from them.

"The look on that man's face," she said. "It was sheer anguish. It made me think—here I've been saying, 'If only Charles had lived another 10 years, if only we'd had more time together, it would have been easier.' But I suppose at any age it's terrible to have it happen. Maybe it's easier for us at a younger age. Maybe we can adjust better than if we were older."

To a certain extent I was adjusting. I had taken hold of my modest "estate" and organized it with an eye to my future.

Because stocks were my husband's choice of investments, I felt I should put most of my insurance money into stocks, although my own savings had been in a savings and loan company with a higher interest yield.

Always poor at arithmetic, I learned to read the stock market page and figure our holdings, but then I devised a better system. My son is excellent at math, so I began taking a monthly reading on our stocks, simply writing down the amount of stock we owned in a company and its price on the first day of the month. Then I would let our son figure our "worth" for that month, good mental exercise for him, helpful to me, and helpful to him because it gave him a sense of usefulness and also a sense of his own property holdings. I leveled with him as to our status. We did not have money for luxuries, but we had enough to meet our bills, and there was no cause for worry as long as my salary continued. In this field, as in my health, I found he needed reassurance. Children worry, more than you think.

There was an amusing side to my financial transactions.

The young man who had been my husband's broker wrote me a note offering his services. I called him one day and said, "I will be having a little money to invest and I'd like your advice. You'll find I'm even more conservative than my husband. I don't want anything that will be a big flash, just a sound, quiet investment with a good interest return."

"Have you thought of Monsanto Chemical?" he asked. "They've been as high as 96 in the past year, but they're down to 44 now. We think they'll be going up and are about at a low now. No guarantees, of course, but I think eventually you stand to make a profit."

I placed an order for 20 shares, and it was purchased at 43⅞. The next day it was 45, and within a week it had gone up to 54.

"Hey," I said to my boss, "I'm a genius. I'm going to quit my job and devote my time to the stock market."

"Don't be too hasty," he said. "They go down as well as up."

The stock did go down, but not as far down as it had been. Meanwhile my son was bugging me to buy IBM, then at 438.

"Dear," I explained patiently, "that is too high per share. If you buy it and it goes up 1 point you've only made $1 whereas if you buy 20 shares of something at $20 a share and it goes up a point you've made $20. Do you understand?"

The next week IBM went up to 496. In one day it climbed 17 points. I tried to keep this a secret, but my son had taken to listening to the business reports on the radio.

"If you'd bought the stock I recommended . . ." he began.

This was the light side. It all helped. Although I felt like the Negro maid, a widow about whose welfare Friend Jan inquired.

"I'm doin' better," the woman said, "but I ain't healed yet."

I was doing better. But I wasn't "healed yet."

CHAPTER 13

Maytime

No WIDOW'S CLOCK AND CALENDAR SYSTEM OF GRIEF is the same. But many of them have told me of a large-scale outburst of sorrow which came three to five months after the death of their husband and served as a climax to the early stage of sorrow, like a crisis in an illness.

Almost five months after Charles had died, Jan had spent a Friday night at our house to attend an entertainment at a nearby church. As I took her home on Saturday morning I gave her a copy of *This Day* magazine in which I had written a column telling of my exalted spiritual feelings the night Charles had died. I thought it would make her happy to read of my conviction of his peaceful passing into another world. Instead I was stricken with remorse to see her at our usual Saturday night gathering, her face still red and swollen.

"I cried all afternoon after I read your column," she said, "but I think it was good for me. It got a lot out of my system."

I felt dreadful, of course. And—because this was before my own experience, a week before in fact—I was at a loss to understand such delayed symptoms of grief. Surely she ought to be "over it" by now.

Tears in public are the thing many widows dread, especially the widow who has been a sensible, unemotional person going into the business world daily with some degree of poise and composure.

And yet, the widow who comes through the difficult weeks beautifully, who stops crying herself to sleep at night and is serene on the surface, suddenly finds herself splashing over—in public.

Jan had warned me that church music made her emotional, and I made a point—and this I continued for some six months—to avoid arriving at church until the musical portion was over. I came to hear the sermon and slipped out as the final hymn was being sung.

But you can't avoid music everywhere. It was the tenth week. May. And I kept hearing the song "Maytime." For some reason it affected my emotions. Why? This song had had no relationship to our lives. It had never been a song either of us was especially fond of. It meant the Municipal Opera, which meant youth to me; the show from which it is taken is a perennial light opera favorite. It is also played a great deal on daytime radio programs in May, I was to find, and now the words took on meaning:

"Sweetheart, sweetheart, sweetheart, will you love me ever? . . . Will you remember the day—when we were happy in May? . . ."

Our courtship had been in May, walking through the countryside around the college town. We had been married in May. May meant wedding anniversaries and Mother's Day.

To widows, one pang occurs when you think that never again will anyone give you exactly the kind of gifts your husband did. The person who lives with you, who knows you better than you know yourself, can—if he is a generous and thoughtful person—bring you delightful surprises. Gifts like the practical whistling teakettle you need, or the silver pin you admired at a shop in a foreign country but passed up because it cost too much (he bought it and kept it as a surprise). The beautiful, expensive, filmy gown in your favorite color or the red flannelette nightshirt with your name embroidered on it; he had sent to a mail order house

85

early in fall to have it for Christmas because it "looked like the silly kind of thing you'd like."

My husband was the one who knew I'd rather have a potted geranium than two dozen cut roses and that I preferred light-pink geraniums to dark-red ones. For Valentine's Day, birthdays, wedding anniversaries there was always a flowering plant. And on one memorable birthday there was a large pile of manure at the edge of my garden with an appropriate card atop it.

All this is why "Maytime" made me cry. Silly, isn't it?

You can flip the switch and turn the car radio off. But one day I was the speaker at a luncheon of 300 women. The part of the program preceding mine was music by a charming vocalist who sang "I Enjoy Being a Girl." It was gay, and I applauded with the others.

"And now for my second selection, a seasonal song —Maytime."

"Oh, dear," I thought. "Ohdearohdearohdearohdear."

The lovely voice poured forth sweetly. The tears welled up in my eyes. My fingernails dug ridges into my palms. Something came to mind. In the early days of widowhood I had read the book *To Live Again,* by Catherine Marshall, widow of Peter Marshall. She had had a similar experience, being moved to tears in public. What was it she had done? Oh, yes, she had concentrated on something—the flowers on a woman's hat.

I found a woman in a flowered hat. Pink. It had seven clusters of pink roses on the side visible to me. 1-2-3-4-5-6-7. Each cluster had three blossoms. And 7 times 3 is 21.

"And now it gives me great pleasure to introduce our guest speaker . . ." the program chairman detailed my history concluding, "She is the *widow* of . . ."

It was the first time I heard the word describing me, and for a moment it threw me. But I took a deep breath. A big smile. "This necklace microphone always reminds me of a funny incident . . ."

It was not the last time I was to experience tears in public. A few nights later I attended the annual dinner at church. A year before, my husband had been elected to the Board of Deacons, a great honor. Now another man was being appointed to fill out his unexpired term. And there was a time of memorial for those members who had died within the past year. We will honor them in prayer. . . . The names were read off.

I bowed my head with the others. And tears began to roll. But this time I was among dear, close friends. I simply reached for a paper hanky in my purse and wiped my eyes unashamedly. And as I looked up, I saw some of my friends looking at me and wiping their eyes too.

Then it was June. A busy, beautiful time of year.

A talented and thoughtful group of friends, the St. Louis Repertory Opera Theater, had suggested giving a concert in honor of my husband. The offer had come in the first onslaught of letters, and I had delayed answering it. It had taken time to set up the program, but finally it was set up for June 11, three months and a week after my husband's death.

The concert was held in Shaw's Garden, on the lawn of the Henry Shaw home. It was a beautiful setting, a beautiful concert, and the weather was perfect. I had expected it to be an ordeal, but I found myself gazing toward the woodland areas and feeling a great peace and calm.

"Thank goodness," I thought, "I've reached the turning point. I'm over it."

The next Sunday was Father's Day. Friends had invited me to come to their house in the afternoon and show some color slides of our trip to Mexico the summer before. I had looked at these pictures on several occasions since my husband's death and was inured to seeing his happy face as he relaxed in a swimming pool at Mazatlan. The picture of the sunset which he had made as I stood by his side no longer brought any sentimental stirrings.

Perhaps where I made the mistake was to pick up another box of slides made on a trip to Mexico five years before. These I had not seen for some time, and somehow the memories brought up proved my undoing.

I returned home, churning inwardly. My son made a comment of some kind—I cannot even remember what the subject was—but I snapped at him. His feelings were hurt. And suddenly I went to pieces. Everything closed in. "How could I cope with life? How could I bring up a son without a father's help? How could I go on? . . ."

And with that, I rushed out of the house, at dusk, and into the wooded area where the little statue stood surrounded by flowers. I knelt beside the stone bench. And then I slid to the ground and lay there, sobbing and beating my fists against the earth.

To me, at that moment, it was life's lowest point.

Looking back, I can see, it was not the bottom of the valley but the crest of the hill. I had passed the crisis.

CHAPTER 14

One Step at a Time

THE DAILY SIDE OF LIFE WENT ON. The meals. The day's work at the office. The shopping.

"Life is just one bar of soap and one roll of toilet paper after another," I thought grimly as I walked around the supermarket.

But things were improving. I realized this was the first time I found myself walking out of the supermarket on Saturday morning with a smile on my face. No longer running for the car to rush to the safety of home, but strolling and smiling.

However, no matter how good you may feel, you can retrogress.

In the beginning I had realized my limitations. My attention span was brief. There are real physical and mental results of shock in the form of loss of memory and mental disorganization, the inability to pull yourself together, to compose a shopping list or a letter, to remember what you said to someone.

But I was doing very well. I had organized my stock "holdings." After some inner debate, I had decided to increase my own life insurance holdings so that, in the event of sudden accidental death, my son would have enough money to complete his education. I who had never "believed in" life insurance had been made a believer.

I was doing fine. Except for one backsliding incident. On June 13 I gave a party to honor the 100th birthday of our old house. We had planned a big bash, a two-day affair for all our friends and neighbors. This was no longer in good taste or practical, but I decided on a small affair, for the Webster Groves Historical Society.

When I was a little girl in first grade, my aunt told me I might invite four guests for ice cream and cake on my birthday. I ended up inviting the entire room. I haven't changed much. On the night before the 100th birthday party, I realized I'd asked casually, by word of mouth, some 60 or 70 or 80 people. Well, nothing to do but prepare for it. I had given many large parties—often we had as many as 200 at Christmas Open House—and I knew how to prepare for mass servings.

I baked and bought half a dozen cakes, and friends brought more. We had plenty of cake. But as I prepared the punch just before the arrival of the guests, I realized with a sinking feeling that there was not going to be enough. I had simply failed to get enough ingredients.

Two couples whose teen-age daughters were helping me receive, in Civil War costumes, arrived first. I confided my fears. In a few minutes the man of one couple and the woman of the other were leaving by the back door and taking off in his car.

"We're eloping," the woman said gaily.

They came back with a supply of ingredients, and by the time the first punch bowl was empty, a replacement was waiting, a replacement far superior to the punch I had made. There was ample for all, and the party was a great success.

But I was embarrassed and chagrined to realize my own inadequacy. Clearly I was not yet back to normal.

I was relieved to observe that my son, whose reactions had concerned me in the beginning, seemed to be taking life in his stride as he prepared to leave for a student tour of Mexico.

I can still recall an incident during the school year.

"Have you seen Daddy in a dream yet?" he had asked.

"No, I haven't." (In fact, a regular dreamer in technicolor and intricate plot in my normal life, I found as a new widow I had no dreams or only a blurred jumble that I could not remember on awaking.)

"Well, I dreamed of him," the boy said. "I dreamed he was sitting in the kitchen when I came home and I said, sort of surprised, 'Oh, hello,' and he said, 'Didn't you hear about me? I'm not really dead.'"

Tenderly I explained that there were two kinds of dreams, dreams of dread and dreams of wishful thinking, things one wished could be true, and that this dream was one of the latter.

However, a week or so later he came up with something a little different.

"I took a biology test today," he said. "I didn't know some of the answers, but I got a perfect score."

"Oh? How was that?"

"Well . . ." he hesitated. "Just as I was wondering about some of the answers, someone seemed to say the words to me. A couple of times they were words I didn't even know, but I put them down and they were right." He hesitated again. "Do you think it could have been Daddy?"

"Suppose it had been?"

"Well, then—he was cheating!"

The response was so typical that I laughed. But I felt a pang too.

One of the greatest needs of the widow is the need for hope—hope for life beyond the grave.

Even the person who has been rather casual about thinking of life after death for herself becomes almost obsessed with the insistence on such a life eternal for a husband or a child who has died. Permanent parting, nothingness for a life that was precious and meaningful, seems unthinkable.

I have heard young ministers talk glibly of the unimportance of such fundamental beliefs as the belief

91

in eternal life. These are outmoded concepts, runs the sophisticated theological thinking.

"We now think of heaven more as 'heaven on earth' —we make our own heaven or our own hell here in this life," one young clergyman told me.

I wonder how comforting such a religious philosophy would be were he to lose his wife in childbirth or his young son through death by accidental drowning. Suddenly the whole idea of "heaven on earth" is a mockery. Our earthly life is a brief span in the eons of time. There must be more to life than this. Surely the person we loved was not created to live such a quick flash of existence, the soul then to be buried with the body.

Other widows told me that as time went on I would sense the presence of my husband more and more. Some women claim to have seen the husband who died.

During the early time of my bereavement I heard of an acquaintance whose son had been suddenly, tragically killed. The father of the boy, a sensible, level-headed, conservative man, not one given to emotional flights of fancy, told of going to his office one night to do some work. He closed the door and walked over to his desk. Then he felt sure he heard the door open and close a second time and that when he looked back he saw his son standing there—one quick moment, but unforgettable and unmistakable.

Nothing as dramatic as this ever happened to me. But now and then, again too often to be a coincidence, there was a consciousness of a presence with you.

This happened to me one day while shopping. It was one of those bad days. A bad day in a bad week. There had been rain and more rain. That entire spring and summer was wonderful for the gardens and the grass but very difficult on the emotions. This particular day I had been hit in the solar plexus again and was down, way down.

"O God," I groaned, driving down the expressway, "You must help me. You've taken away my help. The person I could ask for advice and encouragement is gone. The one who was always there, quiet but unfailing. Now I have no one to lean on. I'm walking alone."

I went into a department store, looking for a list of necessary household trivia. Picture hooks, for one thing. I felt helplessly womanlike. What kind of picture hooks? There were 10-pound hooks and 100-pound hooks. How much did the pictures weigh? Surely I couldn't lift a picture that weighed 100 pounds. I glanced at a man customer, wondering if I might ask him, but he didn't look approachable. Finally I picked out some hooks. Then the decision about paint for the woodwork. Gloss? Semigloss? What had he been using on the trim which I was about to continue to paint? I made my purchase hesitantly and started down the escalator.

All of a sudden a strange feeling surrounded me, a feeling that can only be described as peaceful and loving. As if someone were with me.

"What an odd place to have this happen," I thought. "On an escalator."

Simultaneously, another thought occurred to me: "What a gentle person he had been, so worth loving." That was one of the things I missed most, having someone to love. And yet—I could still love him. Even though he was gone.

The thought excited me. It seemed so obvious, and yet it was an entirely new idea. You can go right on loving the person who is gone. There's no law that says you have to stop loving because he has stopped living.

You can continue to love, and in the very act of loving there is warmth and life for you. You are still alone, yes, but somehow not forlorn, because you are still a loving person.

A Fifth Wheel

THE HINDUS, SO I'M TOLD, HAD A CUSTOM concerning widows known as "suttee." This was the charming habit of tying the widow of a dead man to his funeral pyre and burning her alive. Like Hitler's system for settling the Jewish question, it was a surefire way of settling the widow problem.

There are times in the life of every widow when she thinks with favor of the custom of "suttee."

"I might as well be buried with him," run her thoughts. "It would be easier than being left here alone."

When you have lived most of your life as one half of a couple, there are tremendous adjustments of all kinds. Adjustments to a curtailed income. Adjustments to living for yourself when you have lived for another. Adjustments in buying food, in cooking, in learning to look after the "man jobs" of the house, in being both mother and father to your children, in making decisions by yourself instead of asking the advice of the head of the house.

One of the greatest adujstments for most widows is in their social life. Of all the sad stories I heard from other widows, some of the saddest had to do with the abrupt cessation of friendships which had been a part of their lives.

"We had been meeting with five other couples for 20 years," one widow told me. "Every Saturday night we played cards. The men played one game—usually poker—and the women played something like Michigan rummy. After my husband passed away it made an uneven number. The men sometimes asked an 'extra,' but I could tell they didn't like it. It was easier for them to take in another couple, so I dropped out."

Another widow had been the wife of a prominent executive, the president of his professional organization.

"When we went to the banquets and parties, all the other men asked me to dance and the other wives paid a lot of attention to me," this woman said. "After John died, I was invited to one of the parties but I sat alone, completely ignored. No one came up to me. They were all around the wife of the new president."

"I did not receive one call from a person connected with the big corporation for which my husband worked," said another widow. "Not one call within the year after he died."

"People don't want you around when you're a widow," others have said. "You're a fifth wheel."

It cannot be said too often or too loudly that not all friends are like this. A shining exception is the group to which my husband and I belonged. Originally made up of seven couples, it has had four widows. Each widow continued to come to the Saturday night party. The three "original" couples, Bill and Elizabeth, Bud and Ginny, and Ed and Ginny, called between parties to invite me to dinner. Two of the widows married a second time, and in each case we made much of the ceremony of voting in the new member.

"The Saturday Night Crowd is immortal," I had said flippantly just a short time before my husband's death. "There's Helen's new husband John, and when Helen goes there'll be John's next wife, and when I go Gary will remarry, and then his widow will remarry, and soon the Saturday Night Crowd will have all new names but the parties will go on."

Ironically I had assumed that I would be the first to

go. I had always had this "feeling." Good fallible feminine intuition.

After I became a "loner" in the Saturday Night Crowd, I did my best to cause as little trouble as I could. Since I drive a car and travel extensively on the highway and around town at night, there was no reason for anyone to chauffeur me. The other widow of our crowd did not like to drive at night, so I tried to make arrangements to pick her up or have her drive to my house by day and spend the night, returning home in the morning.

I can never say I felt unwanted, unloved, or a "fifth wheel."

Having been a member of numerous professional organizations, I had many other friends on the fringe of my life, and many of these were to become much closer friends than ever in my sorrow. They invited me to dinner, took me to movies, invited me for weekends out of town, to special big gatherings where they were going in a crowd.

For three weeks in the summer my son went to Mexico on a student tour. I had planned to do many dull household chores during that quiet time alone, cleaning the basement, organizing closets, going through old files, etc. Instead I had not one free evening; the three weeks were a gay social whirl.

I also took to heart the words I remembered my masseuse, Jonesy, quoting: "I said to Mrs. Brown, 'You entertain as much as you did when your husband was alive, don't you?' and she said, 'I entertain twice as much. You have to, to stay in circulation.'"

Another idea came from a widower neighbor of mine. A gardener, he had volunteered to keep some of my choice plants in his greenhouse while I was away, one of the many practical acts of kindness shown me by friends.

"Clarence," I asked when I picked them up, "is it as horrible being a widower as it is a widow?"

"Well," he said, " 'tain't no fun," and then he added with a grin, "until you make some for yourself."

I wanted to stay in circulation, so I set about "making fun" and entertaining, perhaps not twice as much but more than we had done during my husband's illness. Entertaining in our big house had always been a part of our life, and I had always done it easily, serving quick mixes, "store-boughten" fried chicken to large crowds, canned potato salad and bakery cakes. Luckily my finances were not so curtailed that I could not afford the food and liquor.

One area turned out to be much more difficult than anticipated.

In June I was invited to a large cocktail party, a civic event which my husband and I had attended annually. Held at a hotel, it was a lovely party with delicious food, decorations, a good bar, and I decided I would go, alone.

I had some qualms, as I parked the car and entered the hotel, but fortunately I ran into acquaintances in the elevator and we entered together. I crossed the room and was instantly greeted by two couples whom we knew quite well and long. One of the couples moved on, but the man of the other couple volunteered to get me a drink and came back with it.

Just then a woman approached to ask me a question. I replied, looked around, and as if by magic the couple with me had disappeared. Suddenly I had the horrible thought: "They didn't want to be stuck with me."

This may do them an injustice. Perhaps if I had been with my husband they would have moved on or been drawn away as swiftly. But I would never have noticed because he and I would have continued to talk. We enjoyed one another's company at big parties, even liked to sit next to each other at banquets because, in our busy lives, we never got caught up on exchanging news and views.

The rest of the evening went well enough, but I was careful to move from group to group, never wearing out my welcome. I was "looking" for someone, and after a little conversation I would say, "It's been nice seeing you; I promised Dorothy I'd look for her."

I had just left one of these groups when dinner was announced. There I stood alone. Swiftly one of the men I'd been talking to in a group came over: "Peggy and I would like you to sit with us at dinner," he said.

My gratitude was almost pathetic. I said a quick prayer that Peggy (who, I sensed, had instigated the invitation) would never be a widow. But if ever she is, I'll see that she's never standing alone at a big party if I'm there.

A few weeks later I was invited to another big party. It rained early in the evening, and I knew the party was to be held out of doors. I made the excuse to myself that the party would be canceled, although in my heart I knew it would go on. The next day I wrote my excuses and heard from others how I'd been missed. I felt ashamed that I had "chickened out," but the truth of the matter was, I couldn't face another possible rebuff or the feeling of being alone.

Another month passed and another big party, this one a public affair for the press, which meant there might be people I knew well or there might not. Again it was a rainy night, and again I felt tempted to go to bed and forget the whole thing. Lying down, I sensed a headache.

This time, I decided, it was the moment of truth. Either I was to continue going out in public alone or I would crawl in a hole at home and give up this phase of my life. If I gave it up, I was deliberately cutting off an avenue of making new friends. I had plenty of friends, I could rest on my social laurels, but I'd be standing still.

Deliberately I got up, dressed in my best dress, applied makeup and perfume, and got in the car and drove to the midtown restaurant where the party was being held. As it turned out, everyone at the party was a casual, not a close friend, but again I made myself move from group to group, introducing myself if I didn't know the members of the group. When two talented men played the piano, I joined the admiring group standing around.

As I took my departure, a member of the host group came up and squeezed my hand warmly. I knew why. She was a widow.

As I tipped the parking lot attendant, got into my car, and drove home, I tried to analyze the feeling of elation I felt.

The party hadn't been as much fun as all that. All I'd really gotten out of it were some unneeded calories. I hadn't made any great, lasting friendships. I hadn't forgotten my state of widowhood in having fun. But I had survived. I had made myself "go it alone" and carried it off successfully, chin up.

It was a moral victory. Next time it would be easier.

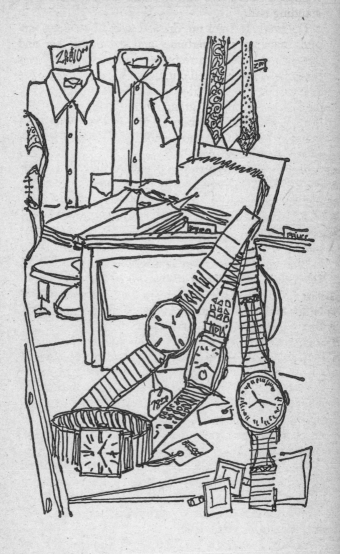

CHAPTER 16

Parents Without Partners

"YOU OUGHT TO GIVE ME A FATHER'S DAY PRESENT," I said to my son facetiously. "After all, I'm being both a father and a mother to you."

It isn't easy. It must be even more difficult for the widow with a number of small children who must be brought through all the discipline problems and shown an example of parental affection and a masculine image.

Our son was 15.

"Your father and I have given you just about all the training we can give you now," I said to him. "You're pretty much on your own from here on out. Either we've done a good job or we haven't but there isn't a lot more basic training we can do."

As is often the case, a lot of his training had been done by others too. He had been a member of the Boy Scouts, in which the leading had been done by many dedicated men in our community. My husband's health was not the best even then, and his interests were not in outdoor life. During his political career he had been away a great deal. So others had provided the masculine image even before his death.

Our son had joined a boys' club four months earlier, and I had attended a meeting of the mothers' auxiliary on that occasion.

"What was it like?" my husband had asked me. "Did you see anyone you knew?"

"Strangely enough, no," I said. "I thought I knew just about every woman in town, but this was a new group. And an odd thing—four or five of them were widows."

"Yes," my husband said thoughtfully, "that must be a great organization for a widow trying to raise a son alone."

What prophetic words. I was to repeat them, tearfully, to the members of the mothers' auxiliary as I took them boxes of his clothing for a fund-raising rummage sale held by the club.

Having a child to care for is a special responsibility for a widow, but it is a special joy too. Grief can provide an opportunity for spiritual growth and character building in a child as well as an adult. It can provide a sensitivity to others in distress which cannot be instilled as successfully in a child who has never known anything but a carefree, happy, insulated life.

There is much help for the widow with children. Such organizations as Parents Without Partners and the Single Parents Clubs are among them. Here the experts can advise the widow—and the widower or the divorced person—on the knottier problems of discipline and control and love and encouragement which face the single parent.

Sometimes it's the little things which cause the biggest problems. For me, shopping for clothes with a teen-age son was a wilderness in which I felt the need of a compass and a map. Oddly enough, my husband had rarely gone shopping with our son; I had done most of the chauffeuring and the advising. But there had always been the court of last resort—should we pay thus and so for a raincoat, or was a special jacket indicated for a special occasion? Now, as in many other things, I was on my own with the total power of decision-making.

I found myself vetoing an expensive watch, tentatively okaying the purchase of a car "if and when," and wondering how my husband would have reacted.

In selecting clothes for a clothes-conscious teenager, I found the simplest solution was to go to an excellent shop geared to the high school and college boy rather than flounder around in department stores, not knowing which rack of size 36s was for young men and which for the retired executive. The prices, I found with traumatic shock, were not much different. At the shops catering especially to young men, I found few bargains but was assured that the styles would be right and there would be a minimum of margin for error. And I found the young clerks sympathetic and willing to do their own share of parental advising— "No, that's too expensive for you at your age. This would be a wiser buy."

Other widows depend on grandfathers, uncles, friends, and I would hazard the guess that one of the attractions of a second marriage for the widow with a son is the hope of sharing parental responsibility again with someone else.

One of the headiest feelings is the knowledge that you are doing a creditable job. When I returned to social circulation and to the land of living, I received a wonderful compliment, which I cherished above any idle flattery about face, figure, dancing ability, intelligence, or personality. It was relayed to me secondhand.

"He says one of the things he likes most about you is your son," I was told.

No one could have said anything that would have pleased me more.

CHAPTER 17

The Blessing of Work

"I THINK YOU'RE SO COURAGEOUS TO GO ON WORKING," a reader wrote me as my column continued to appear regularly after my husband's death.

I read the sentence to the office staff with resultant laughter.

"She has no idea how much more courage it would take for me to quit," I said. "Imagine facing all those bill collectors without a paycheck."

But in all seriousness, the fortunate widow may be the one who is left without sufficient money, who has to continue at her job or go back to the working world in order to survive. Getting up in the morning with a purpose, busying herself with things away from home, carrying on impersonal conversations with people who neither know nor care about her tragedy can be the best possible therapy for grief.

For the woman who has worked most of her married life, the adjustment is minimal. She takes a week or two off for the funeral and the business details and consultations and then returns to office or shop or plant. Her boss may be solicitous and co-workers who are themselves widows may pat her shoulder or squeeze her hand, but for the most part, life goes on and she is back in the mainstream. Evenings and weekends will pose problems, but the bulk of her day will find her the same busy, involved person she has always been.

The woman who has not worked for some time and finds it necessary to earn money has a different problem. She may need professional help, retraining, a refresher course in the kind of work she did before her marriage or before the children came. If she has office skills or formerly worked at a job now in short supply —nursing, teaching, social work—the path will be smoother. If she is just looking for "a job," she may find the easiest way is to visit an employment agency or sign up at one of the agencies which supply workers by the day.

"It's a real adventure," said one widow who went back to office work on a day-to-day basis. "If you don't like one office or one set of bosses, it doesn't matter, because next week you'll be working somewhere else. And it's a wonderful way to stretch your wardrobe. You don't worry about being seen in the same clothes, because you're being seen by different people."

The woman who returns to work after many years may have to prepare for changes. The job seekers' questionnaire is one of them. Where once you filled out a form giving your name, age, experience, and references, now you may be called on to take a battery of aptitude tests and answer questions ranging from your attitude to your father to your attitude toward sex. Rather than bridling and bristling and stalking off, it's better to relax and reflect that these are changing times and the absolute, complete baring of mind and soul via the psychological test to computerized big business is simply another swing of the pendulum.

Some widows have ready-made jobs for them in a husband's business, and some of the most successful adjustments have been made by the woman substitute.

"When my husband died, I spent several weeks getting his real estate and insurance business in an orderly condition so I could sell it," said one widow. "By the time I'd worked in it three weeks, I decided I didn't want to sell it. I wanted to keep it. Besides, where could I make such good money?"

It was an entirely new field for her, but she hired a capable assistant and went to work.

"I recommend it to any widow," she said. "It gave me the most marvelous feeling of challenge and ultimate accomplishment. True, I'd done things in my own home for 25 years, useful things to make my family comfortable and happy, but the things a housewife does, while necessary duties, don't advance her as a job does. It's not the same as having to study and learn new things. When I passed that state insurance examination, I felt as if I'd really done something."

A widow may seek a service job, as housemother in a college fraternity or children's home or institution, as a paid worker in a voluntary organization for which she's worked unpaid for many years.

Another widow may look for a job close to home, in a shop in her suburb. She may examine the artistic talents she's exercised for fun all these years and start a business of her own, doing monogramming, making jewelry, caning chairs, refinishing furniture, braiding rugs, arranging flowers, knitting, sewing. One widow even started a business making clothes for pets.

Part-time selling, especially real estate, is a popular avenue for the widow who wants to keep busy without a regular income but with a possible future vocation.

Continuing education for women is receiving attention at many colleges and universities today, and such courses are made for the widow who wants to improve her skills or simply wants to fill her time, when cultural horizons, stretch mental muscles.

There will be many questions asked by the widow who returns to work.

"Am I too old?" is the first question.

The director of continuing education for women at a large midwestern university says that this question is paramount in the minds of every woman who goes back to school. Interestingly enough, it is asked whether the woman is 33, 65, or, as in the case of one student, 81. The answer is that you are never too old if you have the will to try. The widow should keep in mind that the average woman worker today is married and 41 years of age and that, of the 45—54 age group, more than half of all women work.

The mother who goes back to work has special problems, but there are 10 million working mothers juggling those problems. And the experts reassure those of us who are among that number that the working mother is not the monster she was once supposed to be. It is acknowledged now that it is not the quantity but the quality of mothering that you give your children that is important.

Child psychologists point out that the teen-ager needs a mother who can give love and guidance but also a mother who can let go, and sometimes the working mother is better able to do this than the mother who concentrates entirely on her family.

"My mother was a widow who had to work, but she always had time for us," is one of the greatest tributes children can pay to a mother.

Perhaps the saddest of all widows is the childless woman of means who does not have to leave her comfortable home but finds its emptiness unbearable. For this woman the solution may be a volunteer job with the Red Cross or a hospital auxiliary. If her husband had a lingering illness, hospitals may be depressing to her, but sometimes strength may be found in facing just such a distasteful situation.

"My husband died in the Veterans' Hospital," said one widow, "but I went back to work there as a volunteer the very next week. Somehow I feel as if I'm helping others as he was helped."

Volunteer work, especially aimless, time-filling "busy-work," is not for every woman. Sometimes the woman who does not need to work for financial reasons will do well to take a paid job just the same, in order to give her a reason and a purpose in life. Being paid for a job often bolsters the ego.

And for the widow who does not know where to turn—for work, for interests, for help—there is always her church. There she will find enough activity to keep her busy, enough need to give her impetus, enough love to mend her heart. And more than people at work, she will find God at work.

"No one flies over the Valley of the Shadow," wrote Peter Marshall's widow Catherine. "You walk its rocky paths, step by step."

But taking on a load of work may paradoxically lighten your burden.

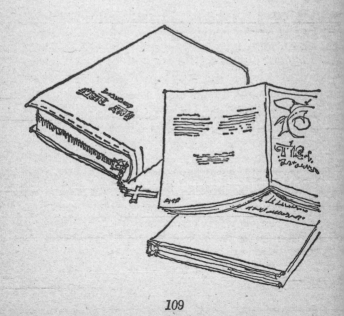

CHAPTER 18

Sex and the Single Widow

CERTAINLY THERE SHOULD BE A CHAPTER IN A BOOK such as this on "Sex and the Single Girl." Or "Sex and the Widow." The problems are not dissimilar, although they are not exactly alike either.

At first the very idea that you might someday feel physical desire for another man is completely repugnant. You are on a spiritual plane, communing with the saints. You are hardly aware of the existence of your body. Sometimes this has its unfortunate side. You put on weight, take less care of your grooming, your clothes, let yourself go. There's no one for whom to fix yourself up.

In my early stages, a widow of longer standing told me, half-laughing, half-concerned, of her experiences.

"I'm starting to have the most idiotic, ridiculous dreams," she related. "They're peopled with half-men, the lower half only. I dream of going through the act, not with anyone my subconscious acknowledges, just a masculine figure. It's all there, the strong arms, the warm flesh. I wake up, gasping and ashamed and miserable."

Her admissions shocked and embarrassed me just a little. Perhaps she needed more outdoor exercise, I suggested. More physical activity. More interests. A leaner diet. Less alcohol. More prayer.

A good friend from out of town wrote to me, asking how I was getting along. Her letter casually mentioned my sex life. I have the carbon copy of my reply, a rather tart one.

"Sex—what's that?" my letter begins. "Who remembers it? Who needs it? For me, at my age, sex isn't something you require like a cup of coffee to wake you up every morning; it's more like champagne for special occasions with a special person, and when the special person isn't there (or champagne is off his diet, as in the case of a sick husband), the desire isn't there either. Or so it has been with me so far. There is no problem because it simply doesn't exist.

"But the other things—the loneliness, the regrets, the remorse, the memories, the lost plans and dreams for the future—it's simply ghastly."

And so my letter went on. It had a high moral tone.

There is no point in being totally autobiographical, but I must admit, in the interests of honesty, that two months later I ran across the carbon copy of the letter, read it, and gave myself a very loud and raucous horselaugh.

For one woman the need for a man, the romantic and/or physical need, will occur sooner than for others, and perhaps in direct proportion to the propinquity of an available male.

When she does start to go out with men, the widow will find the advice books 100 percent correct on one subject. A good-night kiss will turn out to be something quite different than she remembered it from her courting, pre-marital days. A kiss to the young unmarried girl is the peak of the romance, the happy ending, the culmination of her dreams. For the woman who has been happily married for a number of years, a kiss is the beginning, not the ending. Before marriage your instinctive reaction was, "Stop." After years of happy conditioned reflexes, your instinctive reaction, which may take you completely off guard is, "C'mon, let's go."

These reactions are not confined to teen-age widows or healthy women in their 30s. Widows in their 60s have spoken to me of a revived and often disturbing interest in sex.

The happier the marriage, the more the husband was loved, the greater the desire may be. In the widow who sublimated her natural warmth during a long illness, this flare-up may come as a surprise, even as a shock. She thought she had learned to live with it—or rather, without it—and so she had when it was necessary to protect the pride, the dignity, the ego of the other person. Now her question might be: Is doing without sex still necessary?

I remember the case history of a rather well-known widow, Mrs. Michael Todd, better known between marriages as Elizabeth Taylor. She loved her virile, masculine, romantic husband deeply, devotedly, and —according to all fan magazine reports—passionately. The plane crash which killed him left her devastated. A short time later she was finding comfort in a more boyish, less overpowering male figure, the husband of a friend; soon they were married.

Her explanation: "Mike's dead, but I'm not."

To the group of secure married women, such as myself, the remark sounded horribly callous, cruel, animallike.

How many good, respectable church pillars in suburban homes have thought the same thing in their widowhood? Resentfully. Or defiantly. Or excusing themselves.

"He's dead. But I'm not. I'm alive. And healthy. And normal."

"It is better to marry than burn," said St. Paul.

He didn't explain how the 20th-century widow, outnumbering the eligible male 4 to 1, can marry. Or what to do if she burns.

The need for a male, for companionship or copulation, is another thing more easily understood by another widow.

I recall lunching with a friend in the fifth month of my bereavement. She is a maiden lady of 60, but sophisticated and broadminded. We lunched at a bar at a big new riverfront apartment. As men came in, I surveyed them casually.

"I wonder if one of these is the widower some friends of mine want me to meet," I said. "They said he's dark-haired and slightly balding, and I find myself looking at every man who answers that description, and there are quite a few. Of course," I went on, "I'm not really ready to meet another man yet."

"Oh, no, of course not." Her reply was prompt and shocked.

My reaction was to think instinctively, "Kid, you don't know a thing about it. It's been a long, long time."

This is a gray area in which every widow must chart her own course. When to start looking around for a "new man"—not necessarily a marital prospect but an escort.

"I'm hungry for the sound of a man's voice," one widow said.

Working all day with men, dozens of them, I felt no hunger for the sound of a man's voice, but a date, a dancing partner, a man to transform a lone woman fifth wheel into that far more desirable and acceptable social unit, a couple, had great attraction for me by the time half a year had passed.

Long before that I had begun to be aware of men as men in a way I hadn't noticed for years. The milkman, the repairman, the insurance man, any man with whom I did business suddenly became a "man," not just a sexless person with a routine function in my life. At times I felt ridiculously self-conscious. I would offer a lone male visitor a drink, as I would have done automatically during my years as a wife with no thought to the gesture. Now I found myself feeling like the prelude to the big seduction scene in which the temptress slips on "something comfy."

Countless words have been written advising widows to avoid the pitfalls of the romantic interlude. It is easy to see how the perilous situation arises. You may be having an innocent business conversation—being advised by an old adviser of your husband's when he makes a chance flattering remark: "You look cute in those glasses" or, "That's really a sexy dress."

He doesn't mean a thing by it. He's building up your ego. Being a good salesman. Or just being a man and staying in practice at the game. You are a big girl now, and you do not inhale flattery. But you are also a starving woman, and a crumb of attention whets your appetite for more.

You can see how these things happen. How, if the good man were an unscrupulous scoundrel, he could wheedle the widow out of her inheritance. Or how, if it were a little later and you a little lonelier, he could turn from adviser into a normal red-blooded male who sees no harm in widening his experience and performing a needed service for the wife of an old friend.

If you are lucky, the children come in just then or the telephone rings. Or you take a deep breath, stand up, offer him a hearty handshake, and say, "You've been so kind. I do appreciate it. You and your wife must come over for dinner sometime."

There are no rules for the widow; she must make her own. The wise widow would, I should think, confine her social life to men who are marriageable and whom she'd want to marry—even if she doesn't think she'll ever want to marry. Becoming involved with a married man places her among the "100 neediest cases," an object of pity.

The sex drive is a drive, and she can use it in ways other than mother nature intended, to spur her on to creative work, to increased physical activity, to increased concern for the human race. Love for a man is not the only kind of love that brings satisfaction.

The woman who needs to be needed—and that is most of us—can somewhat quench that thirst by answering the needs of others, in church work, in visiting nursing homes for the aged, even in supplying solace to another newer, fresher widow.

When physical love leaves a great unused reservoir of warmth, there is service, there is sublimation. And then, too, there is prayer. Such as:

"Dear God, I do not ask You to take away all desire, because desire is akin to love, and love is positive. But take away the covetousness for another woman's husband. Take away the idle and wasteful daydreaming that uses the resources of my mind. Let me direct my channels of love into other experience, to family and friends and those who may be lonely and cold and need my warmth.

"In the memory of the fine man to whom I was married, let me live up to the highest that is in human nature, not the lowest. And as Christ forgave all sin, forgive my secret thoughts and give me strength to drink the bitter cup of loneliness."

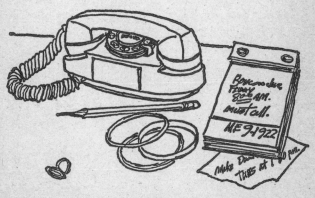

CHAPTER 19

The Years Ahead

WHAT WILL THE FUTURE HOLD? This is the big question to which most widows would like the answer. The philosophical, "Que será, será"—what will be, will be—is not much comfort. The widow wishes she could look into a crystal ball and see a happier day ahead.

Probably if most widows were entirely truthful, they would express a desire to find a second husband. This is true even of those who look horrified at the idea and say, "Oh, no, I could never find anyone to replace dear Murvyn."

"The only happy widows I know," said my widow friend Jan, "are Helen and Louise, and they're married."

Both of these friends are shining examples of the popular song which has it that "Love is wonderful the second time around." It was interesting to the rest of us that in both cases the couples had had mutual experiences.

Louise lost her husband suddenly, in a highway accident. A few days later the office manager at the firm where she worked lost his wife suddenly by heart attack. Louise and Hal, thrown together, found solace in mutual comfort and were married a little over a year later. It was an ideal made-in-heaven kind of thing, and their friends were as happy as they.

Both Helen and John went through long sieges of illness with their first mate—nine years of it in Helen's case, and 29 emergency trips to the hospital. Worn to a shadow by this ordeal, she found her early grief intensified when her only son and his family were transferred across the country. Then, a few years later, she fell and broke her leg. It seemed everything happened to Helen.

Her son wanted her to visit them during recuperation, but she insisted on staying in her own home.

"Don't worry about her," I told the son. "There's a nice young couple, Ted and Bea, who live next door, and they'll look after her. They're just like a son and daughter to her."

They too had had a family sorrow. Ted's mother had died after a long siege. His father, John, a lonely widower, came to visit them frequently. He took to stopping in to see the widow who was bright and cheerful even though her leg was in a cast. He was amused and touched at the spunkiness of this five-footer who told him she was quite capable of getting to the doctor's office in a cab.

"You'll do nothing of the kind, half-pint," John said. "I'm taking you to the doctor in my car."

Well, one thing led to another. At Christmas I noticed the gift of Chanel No. 5 and raised my eyebrows.

"Just a friend," Helen said, blushing furiously. "He's a wonderful, fine, loyal friend. That's all there is to it."

By spring the date was set.

"This is what I got with my broken leg," Helen told her minister as they made plans for the wedding.

"You see," he pointed the moral, "God never sends bad luck without sending something good to make up for it."

"The heart dies many times and is many times reborn," novelist Marcel Proust has written.

You may think the lights in your heart have been turned off forever, only to find them glowing again.

"How can you ever marry again?" an unmarried widow asked one who had remarried. "How can you love anyone in the same way?"

"It isn't the same way," the second widow answered

wisely. "It's like having several children. You don't love them in the same way, but you love them all."

Not every widow finds this happy an ending, but some of the most beautiful romances are those encountered the second time around. A widow appreciates many things about being a wife, not the least of which is the status which a wife enjoys in our society.

"I looked around at the women there with their husbands," Jan said one evening after a big public party we had attended. "They have a certain look about them. A smug, satisfied, secure look. I don't have that any more. I'm unsure of myself, uncertain. I feel like a colt trying to stand on wobbly legs. I don't have a man to tell me what to do, to back me up."

One evening Jan went out with several members of our crowd including one of the men who was a "summer bachelor" and was her escort for the evening.

"Even though it wasn't a real date," she said later, "it was the most wonderful feeling to have a man come to the door and call for me, to open the car door, to adjust my seat at the theater, to put my wrap around me. It made me bask in contentment. This is what I've been missing. I felt like a woman again."

One evening I attended a big community celebration in another town. My hosts introduced me to an attractive man, and I danced a great deal. Later the husband of my friend made a most telling comment.

"You looked so different," he said. "You looked happy. More than just happy. You looked like a bird that had been released from a cage."

"That's what masculine attention does for the feminine spirit," I said ruefully. "There's nothing like it. It's better than Geritol to halt the aging process."

Masculine attention is nice even though you do not hope to marry. And cold statistics tell us that most of us probably will not marry again. There just aren't enough men to go around.

Polygamy has been mentioned, and not entirely facetiously, by world planners concerned over the disproportionate number of women to men.

The widow finds herself viewing this highly nonconformist idea with greater acceptance than she would have done as a wife. "Maybe," she tells herself, "a little polygamy would be good for the institution of marriage as a whole. Competition might force a great many wives who now treat their mates with careless indifference or contempt, to wake up, stop taking a good man for granted, and treat him as the jewel beyond price that he is." Nothing hurts the widow so much as to see her married friends so matter of fact and callous concerning the blessings they still enjoy.

It is an often-quoted rule of human behavior that the happier a marriage, the sooner the bereft person will want to marry again. In many instances this seems to be true but you can hardly make a hard-and-fast rule. Many women might want to remarry but lack the opportunity.

No matter when a widow, or widower, starts to pair up with a new partner, for fun or for keeps, she or he will be criticized in some quarters. It may be five months or it may be five years. Rest assured, someone will say, "My, she certainly got over him in a hurry, didn't she?"

Let them. They have not walked your road in your shoes.

To them the time flew because they were happy. To you the minutes crawled because you were miserable. If you feel you are out of the woods of despair, be grateful for your sound mental health; don't berate yourself for your exuberant physical health and the fact that you are beginning to feel like a human being again.

Most widows still observe the conventional one year of widowhood before remarrying, although in some circles this is beginning to be considered an obsolete and meaningless hangover from the past. Widowers rarely are criticized for remarriage in a shorter time. It's taken for granted that men just can't get along by themselves. Women are the stronger sex.

When to go out, to "return to the human race," is a highly individual matter. In my own case, I began going to parties with friends immediately, to parties in which I was "paired off" with a man in five or six months. The spring had been 10 years long. The summer months flew. A friend of mine quoted someone she had heard—not maliciously, but unhappily. The remark: "She's not grieving much any more, is she?"

"I told her you were putting up a brave front," said my friend, "but that the weekends were rough on you."

"You are so right," I said with a laugh. "Last weekend was especially rough. Two nights after midnight."

But the remark rankled just the same. What do people expect? I wondered. Little does that woman know about dawn on the beach on Easter Monday or the dusk in the woodland on Father's Day or the bottomless pits into which I had plunged between those times, often on the very occasions when I was presenting a smiling face to the suburban scene.

A few nights later I attended a summer band concert, alone, and found myself dripping tears of nostalgia and self-pity as the band played Noel Coward's "I'll See You Again," from *Bittersweet*. As I mopped my eyes and tried to compose my face, I found myself thinking, "Those old biddies should see me now. I wonder if I'm miserable enough to make them happy."

"Forget it," friend Helen said to me. "Remember Aesop's fable about the man and his son and the donkey? You can't please everyone. Don't try."

I also remembered Bernard Baruch's remark:

"Those who mind don't matter, and those who matter don't mind."

Not every widow will necessarily choose remarriage even if the opportunity presents itself. She may find, as the bachelor has found, that a certain amount of freedom can be a heady sensation.

Freedom does not come as naturally to the woman who has been married. It may even be a little hard to recognize at first.

"I'm still putting leftovers in the refrigerator on exactly the same shelves Charles insisted they be on," one friend of mine said. "I've been so thoroughly trained, so brainwashed, that I can't keep house any way except the way I was taught by him."

"I know exactly what you mean," I said. "The cereal bowls had to be placed on the left side of the dishwasher. I'd feel positively disloyal if I put them on the right side now."

It takes a while to get used to your freedom. One night, during a burst of popularity instigated by kind friends, Dolly and Sam invited me to a party on the same night I had accepted an invitation to go out with Julie and Bill across the river in Illinois. The party was a barbecue for June and Harvey back on a visit, and I hated to miss it.

"If I get back in time I'll stop in," I said.

I was driving back nearing their house at 10 p.m. "Are you crazy?" I could almost hear my husband saying. "It's time to get to bed, not time to go to a party."

"Why not?" I asked. And stopped in at the party.

Another evening I was freezing peaches and found myself hurrying at 10 because 10:15 was our bedtime.

"I'd better get to bed," I told myself. "It's almost 10:15."

Then the ludicrous side of the situation struck me. Why did I have to go to bed at 10:15 simply because I always had gone to bed at 10:15?

I finished freezing the peaches, fixed myself a drink, went in the living room, put a stack of records on the record player, and sat up until midnight.

On other evenings I watched the late late show until 1 a.m. Or went to bed at 8 with a good book and flipped out the light at 8:30. No one to whom you had to explain, "No, I'm not sick. I just felt like going to bed early."

There are attractive facets to being alone. You can sleep kitty-corner on a double bed. You can take your vacation any time and any place you want; no need to present a sales talk or wait until the board of directors at your mate's firm royally give their okay for a few weeks away from the job. You can throw out all that old furniture and buy new, have your living room white and gold, and put a dent in the car without accounting to anyone for it.

None of these liberties makes up for the loss of a man for most of us, but they are tiny compensations to living alone.

When will you "get over" your grief? It is a very individual matter. I found myself sorrowing more for others than for myself after a while, because some women apparently find it impossible ever to come out of it.

"They enjoy self-pity. They're playing the martyr," some may say.

I would not be that hasty to judge. Grief is not something you can turn on and off like a faucet. It is also not something you can prolong to please convention. If you find yourself singing a happy song on a beautiful morning, you should not feel you hastily have to assume a long, doleful face because you're a widow.

At church one morning a woman took my hand. "You're such a courageous example to the rest of us. I lost my husband a week before you lost yours."

"I'm so sorry," I said.

Suddenly her tears began to flow. "Whatever are we going to do?" she asked. "How can we go on without them?"

I felt dreadfully guilty because I was no longer in this depth of despondency. Life had resumed its pace. I knew there would be dark moments ahead—Christmas and our son's graduation and perhaps the sight of a grandchild which would never know its grandfather. All of these loomed ahead of me, but I honestly could not say I felt the early despair. It was gone.

This lightening spirit showed itself in many ways. In my early bereavement I had put up a number of photographs of my husband and of the three of us on vacation trips. Now as I woke up in the morning I found myself thinking, "I wish all those people would stop staring at me." I put the family groups away and settled for one nice picture.

On the other hand, another widow told me her only salvation was an album of snapshots of her husband which she carried with her constantly and thumbed through whenever she "felt blue." This would not have been my solution for feeling blue, but to each her own.

"Other widows tell me you never get over it," a friend said. "This I refuse to believe. Something within me rebels. I won't spend my life grieving. I will rejoin the human race."

If there were no other message for widows in the experience of one of our vast number, this would be the paramount one I would like to pass on.

You can surmount your grief. You can rejoin the human race. You may even be a better member of the human race because of your sorrow. You will—eventually—even sense a certain pity for those whose lives have not been touched by grief, for they have not lived life to the fullest.

Our minister, the Rev. Paul Davis, said something of

this in a sermon titled "Lives We Have Not Planned." In it he quoted Irvin S. Cobb, who said, "There is no greater bore than the man for whom everything is going right."

Grief teaches you, he continued, that there are two kinds of people in the world, those who are available and those who are not. You can tell which are open to you by the way they listen when you have sorrow to share.

Christianity, he continued, says we ought to make something out of everything, even defeat. Through sadness, through sorrow, one learns what it is to become vulnerable, and thus one becomes a part of the human race. The prayer of an anonymous Civil War soldier says in part, "I asked for strength, and I was given weakness and thus became strong."

Life is not always easy.

Christ did not have an easy life. For us He endured suffering and death with unselfish courage—and gave us the resurrection.

The strongest of us is but a pale copy of our Lord. But the weakest of women can be a vivid and an inspiring example of how to be a widow.